The
Reluctant
Restaurateur

Imogen Skirving

Polperro Heritage Press

© Imogen Skirving 2003

ISBN 978-09544233-0-8

Published by
Polperro Heritage Press
Clifton-upon-Teme
Worcestershire WR6 6EN
polperro.press@virgin.net

Printed by Orphans Press
Leominster HR6 8JT
United Kingdom

Foreword

Langar Hall is unique because there is no one else in the world quite like its owner, Imogen Skirving. It is an hotel with the memorable combination of great comfort with all sorts of intriguing and delightful idiosyncrasies thrown in; there are charming rooms, a brilliant staff and a lovely setting with a medieval church about eight yards to the south. Add to this, what Bertie Wooster would have described as browsing and sluicing of the highest possible order, and you have something as unique as its proprietor at your disposal.

Imogen presides over it all with an air of mildly perplexed inconsequentiality. You could, for a short time, pick up the impression that it works as well as it does because of good luck and a favourable breeze. Nothing could be further from the truth. Imogen is the most benevolent of despots whose matter-of-fact-air gives the false impression of a genial absent-mindedness. In reality, she is as sharply focussed on every detail at Langar as it would be possible to be and the hotel reflects this. You could not wish for a more amusing and entertaining hostess. Listening to her run through the evening's menu to guests who are about to order shows that she misses nothing and has a great sense of humour to boot.

The staff are delightful too, almost cast in Imogen's own image. Michael, her headwaiter, is a particular gem. Langar was for many years her family home and when you get to know your eccentric host you will soon become aware of her love and affection for Langar. You simply must go and stay there. You will be talking and laughing about it all for months to come and you'll pay many return visits. Imogen and Langar are as unique and hospitable as each other.

Langar has been the home of the BBC's Test Match Special team for many years now and it would be as unpleasant as it would be unthinkable to go anywhere else. For us the Trent Bridge Test Match is made as much by Imogen as events on that loveliest of English Test grounds. How she copes with us all and our combined bad habits I will never know. But she does, and with a beaming smile and just occasionally I find myself qualifying for the ultimate in privileges, which is being asked for a drink with Imogen in the library. This lovely book perfectly reflects all that is Imogen and Langar.

Henry Blofeld
July 2003

Acknowledgements

With gratitude to David Byrne without whom I may never have got around to writing this book. I thank him for his patience and persistence in getting me started.

With apologies to Andrew for turning our home into a hotel and restaurant. Despite the embarrassment this caused him, he has supported me throughout.

With thanks to Jan and Toby for saving me from bankruptcy, and to all the staff who have added to the enjoyment and success of the hotel and restaurant.

With love and appreciation to all my loyal friends and customers for their help and encouragement over the years, not to mention the money they have spent to finance all the improvements at Langar Hall.

While one engages in fulfilling the wishes of others, the fulfilment of one's own self-interest comes as a by-product

The Dalai Lama's Book of Transformation

Contents

INTRODUCTION

Langar Today

Shortly before my father died in 1983, I had the clearest dream. I dreamed that the geography of the house was quite changed, that there were bedrooms and bathrooms in place of passages and flats. Crowds of people of all nationalities were gathered in the hall, lines of expensive new cars were parked under the yew trees in the garden.

I understood that these people had come expecting to meet Lord Byron and Samuel Butler, a distinguished author and philosopher who was born at Langar rectory in 1835, the year this house was built. How could I keep them amused? I awoke in a panic.

*

If I had woken from my dream today, 20 years later, the first thing I would notice is that on a damp September day the central heating is on and the house is comfortably warm.

Steps lead up to a new entrance. On the left, my 1970s kitchen has been transformed into a reception office where, in place of the Rayburn cooker and kitchen table, there are computers, fax machine, a telephone system and photocopier. At the other end where we used to store glasses and china there is a tiny 'Ladies' with two toilets and an antique hand basin decorated with birds and flowers.

Opposite, our old downstairs WC, once visited by Edward VIII when caught short out hunting in the 1920s, is now proudly labelled 'Gentlemen' and boasts a urinal as well as a conventional toilet and Molton Brown toiletries.

The Persian rugs have gone from the stone flagged floors. They could not stand up to the 25,000 pairs of feet that come through the door each year. That includes many parties coming to the restaurant and an army of staff. And what is this discretely built extension in the corner by the study door? A bar! I always longed to pull pints behind a mahogany counter with rows of shiny bottles on glass shelves in front of a mirrored wall. But bars in private houses used to be strictly taboo.

Walking through my kitchen-cum-dining room, I could weep to see how this pretty family room has vanished. Now there is a row of stainless steel sinks, dishwashers and refrigerators, lined up against stainless steel clad walls. There are stacks of cutlery, ugly strip lighting and an espresso coffee machine and water boiler where once Polly the parrot's cage hung.

But look! There is the old dresser, built in the house in 1835, serving its original purpose, storing glasses, crockery and jams. Its drawers are filled with table linen, cloths and napkins, even paper doilies that once would have caused even more disapproval than the bar. I used to steal them from teashops to use as templates for my childhood designs.

A pretty girl in a white shirt and black skirt is making coffee. A young man is taking white wine from a huge fridge. He pauses to fill a shiny bucket with ice from the icemaker, opens the bottle hastily and rushes off towards the dining room. Other young people come in and out stacking dirty plates on a metal table, shouting through to the kitchen:

"Table four cleared!"

They pause at a long hot plate to collect plates of delicious looking food, dashing off with them towards the dining room.

What is going on?

Passing through into the old kitchen, the only remaining fragment of the previous 18th century house where we used to play frantically competitive ping-pong, the ancient stone arches, which once housed bread ovens and spit roasts, are still there. The old stone sinks and wooden draining boards are swept away and there is no sign of the corner cupboard where we used to hide the children's 'gin bottle' and other secrets. The bumpy old ceiling is covered by a huge ventilation system, the walls are lined with large steel stoves, the centre of the room is a bank of table-topped refrigerators and steel shelves rise up to meet florescent lighting on the steely ceiling.

White coated chefs are preparing food, grilling, frying, roasting, steaming seemingly all at the same time. There is a buzz of chopping, butchering, pans sizzling, stock simmering, sauces stirring, bread baking, ice cream churning. Friendly banter between chefs blends in a frenzy of production as the orders come through from the dining room.

"Two cheese soufflés, one terrine, one crab. Two beef, one rare, one well done, sliced, one bass, one partridge - table six!" I hear myself shout as I plonk a small piece of paper under the hot lights.

What am I doing here? And how on earth did the old playroom turn into something resembling the engine room of a spaceship?

Well, it was a long pregnancy and a difficult birth, which I prefer not to remember. I walk proudly though that kitchen now, no longer intimidated by chefs, head chef in my own right although I don't cook any more. There are seven chefs working in the team today of which at least three are 'head chefs.' One working, one off and one 'in the wash' on the same principle as pants and socks. It is an extravagant way to run a kitchen. But I never want to risk being left to cope on my own or let the customers suffer on the head chef's night off. These days I 'go into bat' well padded.

On my way through to the front of the house, I pass the open door of the old Gun Room, a cosy little place where we used to watch television. It is three times larger, but the windows are still the same; there are just many more of them. A party of some 20 people is seated at a long candlelit table. There are flowers down the centre, a mass of glasses half filled with wine and subdued lighting. The diners are evidently enjoying themselves, the noise of their shouts and laughter is so loud that I hope the guests sleeping above have drunk enough wine to knock themselves out, otherwise there will be complaints in the morning.

Following the happy murmur of a crowd of people mellowed with good food and wine, I come to the dining room, the pillared hall, and the centre of the house. Here, our formal family mahogany table, slightly shabby Regency dining chairs, the elegant side board, piano and black lacquer screen, that used to hide the service door, have all vanished. In their place are 12 small white clothed tables at which a seemingly large number of smartly dressed happy people are seated.

How on earth do so many people fit into that small space? And how come everything is going so smoothly? I feel nervous; that old anxiety from my dream hits me again. I want everyone to enjoy themselves tonight and every night and there are just so many things that can go wrong.

A pretty young Frenchman is pouring wine, charming a table of ladies. A girl is clearing plates from another table; there are other waiters in white shirts, silently darting around the room. Michael, our tall, elegant black Maître D' is showing a group to their table, he turns to smile at me, a smile that lights his face and makes me feel more confident.

"Take the order for White Sitting Room one, now, quickly, stop chatting," he commands with such gentle good humour that I scuttle off to see what's going on.

There is something different about the White Sitting Room. It isn't exactly white any more – more a soft light blue grey. The curtains are similar but not quite as pretty as the old ones I knew. The pair of Angelica Kaufman painted tables, that I always said I married for, have gone and the chairs and sofas are arranged around the room leaving a space in the middle showing a large delicate Persian rug. A coal fire burns in the grate more for effect than heat.

Groups of animated people are seated, some with drinks anticipating dinner, others with coffee and brandies. It's pretty crowded and I have to move people out to their table to make room for others to sit down. A complicated version of musical chairs, which fails if anyone refuses to move.

I watch myself as I run through the menu. This is my opportunity to introduce myself to new customers, swap news and gossip with old friends and generally find out who is in the restaurant and why. This is my stage, my happy hour, and my party. This is what makes all the effort worthwhile. When a customer, for whatever reason, wants to change a dish I take note and go off to liaise with the chefs in the kitchen.

On the way I pass the information on to Michael and go off to check what is happening in the Study. Here, time has stood still. At first it looks the same as it did 30 years ago. Bookcases full to brimming with old volumes, untidy heaps of games and magazines, the same chimneypiece, and the same decor as when I was a child. On second glance I see that the large heraldic window has been moved out towards the church to form an alcove. The wallpaper is no longer peeling off the wall where the guttering used to spill over.

The Study is the 'holy of holies'. This is where we hide the celebrities away from their public. Or it becomes a private dining room for parties of ten who are specially favoured, usually because I like them or simply because there is no room in the dining room.

I love celebrities of all kinds. They are invariably amusing, appreciative, easily pleased and provide me with a really good excuse to indulge in a bit of name-dropping.

"These are Paul Smith's photographs. He gave them to me for the bar…"

"Don't disturb me. I'm being interviewed on telly with Janet Street Porter…"

"If I was younger, I'd really fancy Jack Dee…"

"I've fallen in love with Jules Holland's dad…"

And so on, through orgies of swanking.

The grandfather clock at the bottom of the stairs still ticks away with the correct time. Nine o'clock, time to turn down the beds while their occupants are having dinner. Portraits of my husband's ancestors still line the staircase, frowning down at me. When they were being painted my ancestors were finding coal. The landscape of Gedling colliery, the family coal pit, is still there at the bottom of the stairs to remind me.

I hardly recognise the haughty girl in the portrait at the top of the stairs but it's a stunning picture of myself painted in my wedding dress in 1963 by our neighbour, John Townsend. It is often admired although seldom identified with the small plump woman downstairs.

The bedrooms in the front of the house are smarter and more comfortable than at the time of my dream. Apart from the addition of en suite bathrooms, they are recognisable by the furniture and pictures. My father's dressing room, once deep red and masculine, has become a pretty feminine sitting room attached to our old nursery, now called the Brownlow Room and let proudly as a 'suite'.

Going down the short flight of stairs to the wing, I can see that the geography of the house really has changed. There really are bedrooms in place of passages and flats. Just as my dream. It is still a rabbit warren and I would certainly be confused by the elegant new back staircase which has replaced the dark curling worn wooden stairs where asbestos-lagged hot water pipes once crumbled as they carried hot water all the way from the solid fuel boiler up to my mother's bathroom, miles away at the top of the house.

At the bottom of this elegant staircase a new, heavy door leads directly onto a pretty churchyard garden where our pet dogs, cats and even the donkey are buried. Turn right and you walk back into the hall through the new bar. Turn left and you can walk along a new paved path, so narrow that you can touch the house and the church wall without stretching. I am astonished to find that I have even built a new wing. It is not as grand as I would have liked, but the rooms are passably pleasant and the purpose built bathrooms rather better than the ones squeezed into the main house.

The 'wow!' factor is saved for Bohemia where my father used to disappear to paint delightful pictures: still lives and landscapes after Renoir or Monet. Now this large low space has exposed beams on the ceiling and walls, the four posts of the bed, manger-like, are part of the structure. The décor reminds me of the ethnic corner at Dubai airport, a riot of eastern colour and pattern. A bathroom has been added above the old coalhouse. Here a skylight looks up on to the church tower, lines of romantic poetry are stencilled on the walls. An amazing transformation. This is the Saturday night wedding bedroom for young couples who arrive late and fly off again the next morning to their honeymoon.

Outside, the 1920's garage has gone. In the stable yard there is a large hut, a veritable shop which the chefs refer to as the 'dry goods store.' I can't help noticing packets of the best Belgium chocolate pastilles stacked in the corner and stop to take a handful.

Between the wing and the kitchen, the grain house, where the chicken and horse feed was once stored in tall zinc bins, has been converted to the laundry. The kitchen sitting room, where, at the end of the war, I used to enjoy Mrs Malik's Polish beetroot soup, is now a busy office. Here two perky grannies, Jan and Beryl, are working at computers, counting the money, guarded by a cross Pekinese feigning sleep in a basket under the desk.

I walk past and into the stable block to my room. How have I ended up living in a stable? I hate horses! Had I seen this in my dream all those years ago I might not have been so enthusiastic.

There is a bed in an alcove. The bathroom in the saddle room has the old original bath circa 1830 in which, as children, my brother and I used to swim and slither at bath time. I live here in what I like to think, is organised chaos. Shelves of books, boxes of precious papers, unanswered letters. A computer, broken china waiting to be mended, broken chairs, a box of wine saved for someone, a rack of clothes, baskets of undies, big wooden trunks, a massage chair seldom used.

How can I live like that? I don't. I just fall into bed in the early hours of the morning and fall out again five hours later. The rest of the time I live and work in my old home.

Opposite my stable door, the kitchen door makes a convenient short cut to the main house. As I pass, I check the bins for suitable scraps for cats, taste some dishes or stop to talk to the chefs.

Dinner service is over now, the chefs are scrubbing down the walls, stoves and refrigerators, swirling soapy water over the floor and sweeping it out into the yard drains. I drift towards the servery to sort out the end of the dish washing, then to Reception to say goodbye to late leaving guests. Here, in that tiny space where once I spent most of my days keeping warm in front of the Rayburn, a lively lady has been working since three o'clock in the afternoon. It's past midnight.

"Go home. I'll finish the bill," I say, but she refuses my offer.

She doesn't trust me with her computerized billing machine. Quite right. I am far too impatient and prefer to write bills by hand.

Soon the house is quiet. Hotel guests have gone to bed, the last revellers threaded into waiting taxis. Every trace of the night's work is cleared away, breakfast set up ready for the morning. The kitchen hums with the sound of refrigeration, dark and empty. I can feel its ancient character. The staff have gone home, or perhaps to meet up again at some Nottingham nightclub.

I go in search of Roy the night porter to find out what he thinks about aspects of today's news or swap information from the latest books we are reading. He reads history or biographies and I enjoy our intense discussions. We agree on the glorious past with a seasoning of gloom and doom ahead. Two cups of tea, the ritual of filling my hot water bottle; I turn off a few forgotten lights, leave notes for the morning and retire to my bed in the stables.

I can't think how, but that dream came true. And, I must admit, I am living in a way to which I am very pleased to have become accustomed.

CHAPTER ONE

Langar Hall's Past

Langar Hall is steeped in history. The name Langar means a place of pilgrimage, which may explain why the village church of St. Andrew is exceptionally large. Built in 1200 to house the multitudes of pilgrims visiting the Saxon priory of St Ethelburgers between Langar and Colston Bassett in search of healing and remission for their sins. The 16th century Langar Hall was attached to the church for the convenience of the noble families who lived here. They could attend daily mass without 'catching their death' as they had in the time of the plague when the first Langar Hall was situated one mile away to the north, on the banks of the River Smite.

For 200 years, the Scroope family owned Langar. It was their family home, halfway between their main Yorkshire estates and London. If you draw a line from Edinburgh to Greenwich, it passes directly by the moat and through the reception entrance. This is the Greenwich Meridian line and probably a 'power' line too. The Scroopes were a powerful Catholic family, lords of the north, Chancellors, Archbishops, King-makers and one, a close friend and alleged traitor of Henry V, is immortalised by Shakespeare in a speech by Henry V:

> What shall I say to thee Lord Scroope? Thou cruel
> Ingrateful, savage and inhuman creature?
> Thou didst bear the key of all my counsels
> That know the very bottom of my soul…

There might have been some misunderstanding here. But this Lord Scroope was executed and his head paraded through England from south to north before the battle of Agincourt.

Emmanuel, the last Lord Scroope of Langar, was a gambler who avoided paying the taxes levied by Cromwell and lived to have the debt cancelled on the return of the monarchy. He played little part in politics, thus saving his house from being razed to the ground. There is an account of Lord Scroope's men on parade one misty morning in the 1640's, ambushed by Roundheads from Colston Bassett and all slain. I disturbed a mass grave when laying new drains in 1991; skulls of young men with good teeth of that period were found together. We buried the bones in a communal coffin, with honour and ceremony and their souls do not trouble us.

Emmanuel Scroope married Elizabeth, daughter of the Duke of Rutland. This marriage added acres to the already large estate at Langar. Elizabeth sadly had no children but her husband's mistress, Martha Jeans, bore him five illegitimate daughters. The eldest, Arabella inherited Langar Hall with 10,000 acres and married John Howe, a young politician from Gloucestershire who was a favourite at the court of Charles II. He persuaded the king to legitimise his wife by Act of Parliament. Thus Arabella assumed all the rights and titles befitting a lady of her station.

Arabella and John Howe were the founders of the great Howe dynasty, one of the most illustrious families of 18th century England. In the reception area at Langar Hall today there is a reproduction of Gainsborough's great portrait of Lady Howe, wife of the Admiral, and there are sepia sketches of the house and prints of Admiral Lord Howe around the house. At the end of a long career in the navy, he led the British fleet to victory over the French on the 'Glorious First of June' in 1794. We mark his victory with a celebration at Langar Hall every year.

The great house, far larger than the present more modest farmhouse, stretched out into the field, overlooking the ornamental moats. The Howes 'modernised' the Elizabethan house, enlarging it and adding an elegant pillared façade looking west over the deer park. After the death of Admiral Lord Howe in 1798, his daughter Sophia and her husband stripped Langar Hall of its treasures and broke up the estate. The house was deserted, then sold in 1818 and demolished. Only fragments remain.

On the lawn in front of the house are two stone balls, which once topped some ancient gateway. They now rest on the bases of two of the six Ionic columns from the 18th century portico. These give an indication of the vast proportions of the old Langar Hall at the height of its magnificence.

The present house was built on a fraction of the site in 1835 incorporating a fragment of the kitchen wing, a few old doors and some masonry scattered in the garden. Nothing else remains

At the time the present house was built, Thomas Butler was rector of Langar. His son Samuel was born in 1835 and grew up to be a philosopher, artist, author, friend and rival of Charles Darwin. In his autobiographical novel The Way Of All Flesh, he describes his sad childhood at the rectory with vivid descriptions of Langar (Battersby on the Hill) and its inhabitants. Professors of English literature from all over the world come to visit the village and marvel at the gracious old rectory that has hardly changed since Samuel Butler's day.

My great-grandmother, Annie Bayley, bought Langar Hall in 1860. She was the daughter of the composer Henry Farmer (who wrote the Harrow School song) and married Thomas Bayley, a wealthy coal owner and Liberal MP for Chesterfield. He built her a fine house in Nottingham but she eventually left him to his career and their teenage children to their follies and moved to Langar.

She would have travelled by train from Nottingham to Barnstone station, a mile from Langar, and then by horse and carriage to Langar Hall. Her family frequently cycled from Nottingham to visit and, in time, the scandal of her separation from her husband and escape to the country was forgiven and forgotten. Life at Langar healed the wounds and her husband, Thomas Bayley, retired to spend his last days here. He and Annie are buried in the churchyard under the shade of a sycamore tree.

In her will, Annie Bayley left Langar Hall to be divided between her four children. My grandmother, Muriel, was the only one who wanted to live here but, as she did not inherit the wealth of the Bayley coal mines, she was obliged to sell most of the land to buy out her siblings (just 30 acres surrounding the house today).

Muriel married Percy Huskinson, an engineer and one of ten sons from Epperstone. Percy ran the first buses in Nottingham but his company did not survive the legislation obliging all motor vehicles to be escorted by a man on foot waving a red flag. He owned the first garage and showroom in Nottingham with the concession to sell Daimler cars but, with growing competition, he gave that up and retired to lead a modest life with Muriel at Langar. He founded the Scout organisation in Nottinghamshire while Muriel started the local WI. They had two sons, my father Geoffrey, and his younger brother Leonard, an artist and illustrator.

My father, Geoffrey Huskinson, inherited Langar Hall on the death of his mother in 1933. He married Carmen de Las Casas, a descendant of Napoleon's friend and secretary during his imprisonment on Elba. Her father, a Spanish grandee whose ancestors arrived in Cuba with Christopher Columbus, came to England as a young man and made his name playing polo with astounding success. Shortly after her marriage, my mother's family house near Taunton was demolished. She saved the Robert Adam pillars there and had them brought to Langar Hall where they transform the dining room, lending it the air of grace and elegance that it has today.

CHAPTER TWO

Childhood At Langar

I was born on August 19th 1937. That year my father's Gedling Colliery was amalgamated with the Seely colliery at Calverton to form the Digby Colliery Company. This probably saved my father from impending bankruptcy. He always insisted that my birth had brought him good luck. A large new pram, which I still have, was bought for me and Nanny Laing was employed to look after me and my elder brother Mark.

I was christened in what is now the White Sitting Room and was named Imogen after my maternal grandmother. It's an old Cornish family name: Imogen is the heroine of Cymbeline, Shakespeare's play about the Cornish kings. Although Langar church was originally joined to the house and my father was a regular attendant, in those days Catholics were forbidden to set foot in a Church of England. My mother was a staunch Roman Catholic who believed she would burn in hell if her children were not brought up in the Catholic faith.

Mark and I lived with Nanny in the nursery (now the Brownlow Room) and slept in the night nursery (the Nursery Room) with nanny's room across the passage but no one was ever allowed to enter her room. Nanny was immaculately clean and tidy; she wore a blue cotton nurse's dress with white cotton bands to hold up the sleeves and a white apron. She cooked our meals which we ate with her upstairs in the nursery. The plates and cups were a Harlequin set of different colours. My plate was pink, Mark's blue, the lilac cup and plates were Nanny's and no one else was ever allowed to drink from her cup or eat from her plate. She never touched animals and we were only allowed to play with them in the garden or 'downstairs'. Every morning, in all weathers, Mark and I were sent outside 'to play'. We made 'houses' in the yew trees where we played with our imaginary friends. In the afternoon we walked to Barnstone, me in my big smart pram with Mark dragging along behind. We called on Mr Daft at the Post Office on the way and when we were old enough to go off on our own, we made expeditions to scary Mr Moony who kept the shop in Langar.

Every afternoon at four o'clock, dressed in our best clothes, we visited the grown-ups downstairs in the study which has hardly changed to this day. We had to be quiet, sweet and careful. If we got too excited or didn't 'behave' we were sent packing back to the nursery. This was no hardship; it was our 'place' where Nanny was always kind and understanding. We loved her. With Nanny we felt safe.

My father travelled to work by train from Barnstone to his offices in Derby Road, Nottingham, where I once found him playing ping pong over two desks joined together with a net in the middle. His business partner Jimmy Seely introduced him to hunting and on winter Saturdays he and my mother hunted with the Belvoir. They had a groom called Herbe who polished the tackle in the saddle room (now my bathroom) and kept the hunters in the large stables either side. As a treat he would take us out in the smart black and yellow pony trap, trotting off at a spanking pace, calling on friends around the vale. My mother, brought up with horses in the Westcountry, was an excellent horsewoman. She explained to us that she preferred horses and dogs to children and found it difficult to show us the same affection. We took this for granted and were neither upset not expected any different.

Coming from a Nottingham industrial family, my father had little riding experience. He was an all round sportsman. He played rugger for the Harlequins and once for England. He played tennis well enough to put in an appearance at Wimbledon and to be invited to all the best tennis parties. But his passion was cricket. He played for Nottingham as an amateur in the 1920s and later became president of Trent Bridge Cricket Club. He frequently entertained many famous cricketers at Langar Hall when test matches were played at Trent Bridge. Don Bradman, Douglas Jardine and C.B. Fry would play cricket after dinner in the hall, using the front door as a wicket while my mother fielded frantically to save the glasses on the table. As a proud member of the I Zingari he toured with them playing cricket every weekend in the summer. Immediately after the war the I Zingari and the Dutch cricket X1 went to Berlin on a peace playing tour. It's hard to believe, but I remember how shocked he was after seeing the ruined city and telling us about the rats.

My parents' life together was pleasant during those few years until the outbreak of the Second World War. I can see myself on the lawn on my little wooden swing one hot summer's day. Nanny came rushing out of the French windows calling to my mother: 'War has been declared. I've just heard it on the wireless.'

At first there was little change in our routine nursery life. My father, who served with the Grenadier Guards at the end of the First War, joined his local regiment, the Sherwood Foresters. With Herbe and Bill Crowe, the gardener, he was called up and after months of training, they went off to the war. They came home unexpectedly from time to time when great excitement was all too swiftly followed by tears of parting.

The wireless became the centre of nursery life. A large wooden box with a gold cloth front and big buttons which moved through a series of squeaks and whistles until the voices become clear, it stood on top of a high chest of drawers. Mark and I stood on the half opened bottom drawer to listen to *Dick Barton - Special Agent*. Nanny listened to *Workers Playtime*. The news was the highlight of the day.

In my father's absence, my mother took over the responsibilities of running Langar and the necessity of providing for the household. She spent more time in the nursery and I think she was happier in the role of chatelaine than as 'county wife.' She never liked parties and hated entertaining. Left to herself she became a very strong woman and by the end of the war there was no question who 'wore the trousers' in our family.

My mother loved to work in the garden, She kept hens on the tennis lawn, pigs in the barn, ducks and geese on the moat. Tom Smeaton, a grumpy old Scot too old for war, helped her. He kept sweets in his apron pocket and lived with his wife at Church Cottage where Mark and I loved to be invited to tea. Mrs Smeaton made mouth-watering lemon curd tarts. Tom grew mountains of vegetables in the walled garden. Nothing went to waste. Apples were carefully stored, plums, damsons, pears and crab apples were bottled or made into jam. In August we went on blackberry picking expeditions to the Belvoir hills. Blackberry and apple pie is still my favourite early autumn dessert. Mark and I collected the milk from Mrs Selby, bringing it carefully home in cans. We podded peas and beans and generally played our part in my mother's successful 'self sufficiency' wartime programme.

Once, and only once, Mark and I hid and watched what was happening when the men came to kill the pig. The poor pig was caught and carried screaming into the yard. A quick gun shot was followed by oceans of blood, saved in a bucket, for black puddings. Old Mrs Crow came for days of frantic cooking. She used every bit of the pig for sausages, scratchings and other delicacies. The joints of pork were shared with our neighbours and pork was on the menu for days. The bacon sides were cured and hung in the larder that is now the servery between the kitchen and the dining room. Today this is the busiest place in the house where we carry the plates to and from the kitchen, make coffee, wash up and do all those things connected with the restaurant service.

The first refrigerator did not arrive until the 1950s and lasted for 25 years. Shopping was done at the kitchen table where the salesman from Hardstaff & Brown in Bingham would take our weekly order, crossing off the coupons in the ration books. Eggs were kept in isinglass in a bucket in the larder along with the bacon and Kilner jars of preserved fruit. Food was precious. Nothing was left to waste. Sweets were treats kept in a tin in the nursery, one after lunch and then only if we had left a clean plate.

I still save scraps of food. Bits of butter go back to the kitchen, bread for crumbs, birds, ducks and chickens; left over bits of meat and fish for cats. If I catch young staff throwing useful scraps into the bin when they clear the plates I tell them about the butter ration. 'Don't forget the cats' is a familiar cry even on the busiest night.

Langar airfield was built on the Harby road over prime grazing land which, with its low hedges, was a favourite 'run' in the Belvoir hunting country. Lancaster bombers were serviced there. They flew in low over the house, the noise of their engines rattling the windows, sometimes limping in for repair, ready for another raid. I still find the sound of aircraft comforting.

The house was camouflaged with ivy. I was terrified of the huge moths that lived in the tenuous branches and flapped round the nursery light. The moths today seem tiny by comparison. Certainly there are very few of them since the ivy went in favour of the present colour wash.

Wartime at Langar was safe and exciting for children. Despite the imminent expectation of the Nazi invasion we were never made to feel afraid. But during our long mornings in the garden, perched in our ' houses' in the yew trees, Mark and I used to imagine what horrors might lie in store and made plans to escape if we were captured.

In some ways it was a safer world than today. Distant Hitler was a greater threat than a burglar. The house was never locked, the car was left with its keys in the garage. Who would want to steal it? There was too little petrol to get very far. We had Mickey Mouse gas masks, Nanny had a tin helmet and with my mother joined the Women's Home Guard. The cellar became our air raid shelter but to my great disappointment there were only a few nights when we were bundled out of bed to sleep there in bunk beds with the mosquitoes. One morning we rushed out to find the shrapnel from the only bomb dropped in the field in front of the house.

Hitler played a large part in our reality and one night I had a very disturbing dream that has stayed with me all my life. I dreamed that Hitler marched up the drive ahead of a large army. My mother, old Tom and Nanny, wearing their tin helmets, armed with guns and sticks, stood in a line outside the old garage, ready to fight. I broke ranks and ran towards Hitler, inviting him in for tea. In the morning, I was so ashamed of this dream that I never told anyone but I often remember it when German guests are staying. My philosophy has not changed. I regard everyone as an individual and I'm sure that if Saddam walked in tomorrow I would still try that old adage: 'If you can't beat them, join them' and offer him tea.

A series of refugees from the London blitz arrived, traumatised and nervous. They were more frightened of the country or possibly my mother, than the bombs in London and returned home as soon as they recovered their health. Only twins, Ronnie and Robbie stayed. I loved them like baby brothers and bossed them around mercilessly.

The arrival of the American Air Force at Langar airfield brought more excitement. The men threw packets of chewing gum for the children as their trucks rolled through the village. Nanny said the gum we brought home was poison dropped by Hitler and she would not relent. She made me a party dress from a silk parachute given to us by Gadoba, one of the nurses who often came to the house. All the village was invited to the Christmas parties in the camp. There were games like musical chairs and blind man's buff and wonderful things to eat called candies.

We were sad when the 'Yanks' left. Their barracks was taken over by German prisoners of war. Ernst and Hans came to work in the garden every day bringing tuck boxes with their lunch which they ate in the pantry (now Reception). They made cocoa from lumps of chocolate. I would hang around waiting for a crumb but even grated and mixed with sugar it was too bitter. They grew smoking tobacco plants in the flowerbeds, dried it, cut it and rolled it into cigarettes. Ernst married a local girl and stayed in England after the war. One day many years later his grand daughter came to a wedding at Langar Hall. I wish he had come too as I would love to have met him again.

Mark and I longed to go to the village school but my mother insisted we attended the PNEU evacuated from Nottingham to Whatton. She drove us half way in a Morris 8 to meet the vicar's wife (who had more petrol) at the Granby junction. I always felt sick in the back of the car, arriving at school in a miserable state. Sometimes, when the car broke down, my mother took us on the back of her bicycle which was worse than the car journey.

One day my father returned from Dunkirk. He was stone deaf from the bombing on the beaches and never recovered his hearing. His first hearing aid was a big ear trumpet attached to a leather battery box that he plugged into on waking and carried around all day 'tuning in.' Typical of his generation, he made light of the horrors he had been through, preferring to see the funny side, making jokes against himself and telling very funny stories of his experiences. Quoting from an old children's book he would sing:

> The elephant when he was wounded
> Ran faster than the big baboon did.

After Dunkirk my father commanded the 9th battalion of the Sherwood Foresters and among his duties was the organisation of the Nottinghamshire Cadet Corps. We visited his camps around the county. At Rufford park I was most impressed how they washed the pots in sand. Each summer there was a camp at Langar when the church field was covered with tents. Each time I heard the bugle call 'come to the cook house door boys, come to the cook house door' I rushed off to be the first in line for lunch. Bully beef and mash was my favourite.

Towards the end of the war, Nanny packed her bag and went to look after my aunt's new baby. Outside her room by the steps, I clung to her crying. Somehow I knew she would never return. The train journey to Taunton was long and crowded, she collapsed haemorrhaging and ended up in the Derby Sanatorium. During the seven years she had looked after us no one realised that she had TB and, thanks to her high standard of hygiene, none of us caught it from her.

I saw Nanny Laing once more before I was sent away to school. She was sitting up in bed on a veranda at the sanatorium in the freezing cold. She died at the age of 37 during my first term at school and is buried in the family plot in Langar churchyard.

Nanny had been our world, our protection, her nursery our refuge. From now on Mark and I were on our own and constantly in trouble. My mother was known as the Pope's Sergeant Major, and if Mark and I did not obey her, shades of her ancestors' Spanish

Inquisition clouded our days. We learned to live with it. My brother Mark used to make me giggle so much at those dreaded meal times that I was constantly expelled to my room for being 'impertinent.'

My dear sensitive, day-dreaming brother Mark was deaf. Instinctively, I had been his 'ears' until he was sent away to a school run by monks at Gilling Castle in Yorkshire. He was quite happy but I missed him and Nanny dreadfully. A very different new nanny came to look after our baby brother when he was born. She didn't cook and we were no longer welcome in our nursery. I found my mother's cooking unpalatable. I can still smell the 'grey' Sunday joint boiled up on Monday with parsnips. Rice pudding, tapioca and sago served with jam were the worst. Whatever I did not eat at lunch was served again at supper so I used to put my food in the cupboard when no one was looking. That cupboard is still there to the right of the fireplace in the Indian Dining Room.

I dreaded each mealtime. Even the smell of frying fat bacon in the morning made me nauseous and I was always in trouble for being a 'faddy' eater. Roast chicken and salad, jelly or bread and butter spread with hundreds of thousands was all I liked to eat. Perhaps this is the reason why I am so passionate about good-tasting, fresh, edible food today.

A few weeks after my eighth birthday I was sent away to St Mary's Convent at Ascot. I was so small for my age that even Harrods had difficulty finding a uniform to fit. Navy tunic with matching pinafore, blue blouse, liberty bodice, navy knickers with white aertex linings, brown socks and shoes. Packing the trunk was exciting and I was really looking forward to going to school. We made the journey to my uncle who lived at Stanton Harcourt near Oxford. The next day he drove me to the Convent in his yellow open 1924 Rolls Royce of which I was unaccountably ashamed. He left me and my school trunk at the front door in the care of the nuns.

The nuns were kind but I felt so lost and shocked that I cried constantly for four days. Years later the nuns told me that they were about to send me home when I cheered up. I never looked back. I loved everything about school especially the food. Roast lamb and chocolate roulade, creamy milk from their Jersey herd in miniature bottles drunk through a straw in the grounds at 11am. The nuns saved their food rations for the children. It was a great improvement on home cooking.

We slept in cubicles in a dormitory. Mother Dominique sang us lullabies before we went to sleep. We attended Mass every morning at 7am and Benediction in the evenings. For church we wore black veils during the week and white on Sundays. I loved it all and determined to be a lay nun when I grew up. Those were the nuns who cooked, cleaned, served and doled out spoonfuls of Radio malt after meals. In a strange kind of way there were many similarities in my later life.

I made lifelong friends with other girls my own age whose parents, living closer to Ascot, took me out from school one weekend a month. Whenever I could get permission I stayed with them in the holidays. My friends were not so keen to stay with me at Langar. I think they were too frightened of my mother. She was strict and I am grateful for that because I certainly was not spoilt and, expecting the same discipline to apply away from home, I soon discovered that life 'outside' was pure delight.

By 1947 my life at Langar had changed irrevocably but I still loved the place so much that I used to take a jar of earth from the garden and a bottle of water from the moat back to school with me where it would sit in my locker like some mystic charm until the long months passed to the school holidays.

After the war my Mother had two other sons. I was the only girl in our family of four children. Life revolved around my two younger brothers and I took up the responsible role of bossy elder sister. Mark was always in trouble and remained the 'black sheep' of the family for as long as my parents lived.

He excelled at art but after being expelled from Edinburgh Art College, he was deported to New Zealand where he revelled in the freedom of sheep stations and we lost touch for several years. After a chequered career, he is now a very successful artist who may have already achieved his ambition to see his sporting cartoons hung in all the best country house loos in England. I love to sell his rude cartoons in reception, posting off the money so that he regularly gets a nice surprise at breakfast. We are very close and he still makes me laugh. Our lunches together last into the night when his dear, long suffering wife Judith drags him home, just a little tipsy.

My father planted many trees and created a 'hanging garden of Langar' with terraces running down the north slope. Bill Crowe grew perfect vegetables in regulated quantity. He won every prize for sweet peas and kept bees for honey and to pollinate the apple trees. There were tomatoes, grapes and house plants in abundance from his heated greenhouse. He mowed the lawns on a huge Dennis mower and in the winter months kept the fires going and did all the necessary painting and decorating. I wish he was still here; I miss him every day.

In the winter holidays we spent days tobogganing down the hill in the field in front of the house or skating on the moat. There were rather wild Exmoor ponies to ride that always ran away with me so I did not like riding at all. Hunting was my greatest dread.

One Boxing Day, after the annual meet at Bingham, my pony bolted up the long drive to Wiverton Hall. I threw myself off at the feet of Field Marshall Lord Montgomery who was staying there as the guest of Major General Sir Miles Graham, one of his staff officers at Alamein. The house party, returning from the

Langar Hall 1792

Langar Hall c1900

Langar Hall 1900

Langar Hall interior 1900
(now the bar area)

Langar Hall 1910

Langar Hall 1915

My grandparents Percy & Muriel Huskinson

My parents, Geoffrey and Carmen Huskinson
on their wedding day

My parents in the garden at Langar Hall

With Nanny 1940, and below with
my brother Mark

meet, were just getting out of their Rolls Royce when I performed my spectacular fall.   After that episode I was excused from hunting and eventually from riding altogether. This was a small price to pay for being labelled a 'sissy.'

I was also bad at games while all my brothers excelled at cricket. They practised with nets on the croquet lawn while I spent hours reading in my room (now the Lilac room) but I could not avoid those tedious afternoons watching them play in cricket matches all over Nottinghamshire & Derbyshire. The only escape was to help with the teas in the pavilion - good training for being the best and fastest sandwich maker in the Langar kitchen today.

I left school when I was 15, having done much better in the exams than expected. My friends all went on to the sixth form and passed their entrance exams to Oxford. Convent girls were notoriously wild in those days and my closest friends were all 'sent down' for bad behaviour before the end of their first year. I was sent to the nuns' Domestic Science College at Ascot, next to the Convent where I learnt the basics of cookery, how to iron shirts properly and to make my own clothes. Being too small to buy dresses in the shops until Mary Quant made tiny clothes years later, this immediately proved very useful.

I didn't excel at housekeeping and to this day I have a Buddhist approach to spiders and cobwebs. Even wearing glasses I don't notice dust, but give me a shirt to iron and I'm happy. Food and cooking became a way of life.

CHAPTER THREE

Growing Up

In 1950 my mother bought a house in Ireland: Waterloo Lodge on the banks of Lough Derg, County Tipperary. We used to go there in the school holidays. Four children and our school friends, two Irish servants, one governess, three dogs, my hamster and budgerigars in a cage. We took the train from Derby to Liverpool then the overnight boat to Dublin. Lunch at the Hibernian hotel, and then the train to Nenagh where we were crammed into various local cars for the final journey.

There was no food rationing in Ireland and sweets were plentiful which for me was the great attraction. We bicycled to the village to stock up with pink and white sugared caramels which we ate in a pine wood by the lake on the way home. This was my first experience of food in abundance; there seemed no limit to the cream and butter and Irish home-made soda bread. I spent a lot of time helping in the kitchen.

The grown-ups started drinking at eleven in the morning. Gin and sherry or gin and ginger beer. After a rest in the afternoon they started again when, at 25 minutes to six 'the sun was over the yardarm.' My parents were not alcoholics but like many ex-pats they were bored and drank too much. Consequently I am never phased by drunks; indeed I find I am so tolerant that I hardly notice anything untoward. It was great training for a future restaurateur.

I learnt to drive on Irish country roads where the traffic was mainly cows and pony traps. There was no driving test. The licence was bought from the Post office and off we went, Mark cheerfully volunteering for every errand, never reporting the scrapes which occurred.

We learnt to sail in my father's boat The Bawneen which had concrete ballast and faded red sails. It was said to be unsinkable but when hit by sudden squalls it was quite scary. After a while I chose to stay behind and learned to milk the cow. During rare heat waves we swam in the muddy water and took part in local regattas where we made friends with other children. On rainy days we sat by the peat fire playing long games of canasta or bridge.

It was heaven for children but when I left school I spent months there on my own with my parents and I was lonely. I passed my time devouring books, historical novels and biographies. I claim to have read War And Peace in a week. When I wasn't reading I cooked. Geordie, who lived on an island nearby, encouraged me: for my 16th birthday he gave me Madame Prunier's Fish Cookery Book. Its black and white pictures filled me with delight. I spent hours making quenelles de brochet from huge pike caught on nightlines set in the lake. I still use the recipe but, unlike my first attempts, the pike mousse on the menu today is, well, it's different.

To avoid spending any more time in Ireland, I found myself a job selling toys for Christmas at Redmayne and Todd. I caught the 7.30am bus to Nottingham every morning and the 5.30pm bus home. I loved selling. I loved being a member of staff. Work experience was fun.

At the weekends I cooked. Elizabeth David wrote a weekly column in the *Telegraph* which I followed religiously despite my mother's complaints about the cost of a lemon at six old pence and criticism that the food was 'messed up'. I liked it and nothing was going to put me off.

When my parents returned to Ireland, I refused to give up my job and stayed behind at Langar Hall. Freedom at last, but at a price. It was quite frightening coming back to the dark empty house at night, walking up Church Lane, running past the churchyard until I reached the safety of the kitchen door. Bill Crowe the gardener saw that I was 'all right' but apart from his visits I was completely alone.

Eventually I was sent to London to the Constance Spry Cordon Bleu School of Cookery in Marylebone Lane. I had lodgings in Trevor Street opposite Harrods with Madame Manley. She taught French during the day in her elegant first floor sitting room where, it was rumoured, she had taught Winston Churchill. She employed an excellent French cook, and dinner was taken together with her and the other lodgers in a formal dining room in the basement. When I stayed in London at weekends, Mrs Manley included me in her social rounds, frequently taking me to tea at Claridges with her friend Princess Alice. They were both very deaf and complained that they could not hear the music and 'would the band please play louder!'

One day my father took me to lunch at Madame Prunier's in St James Street; afterwards we wandered into Christie's where an Old Master sale was in progress. I watched with rising excitement as a triple portrait of Charles I by Van Dyke fetched £11,000. I was hooked. This was the start of my lifetime fascination with art, especially art and money. After that I played truant from the cookery school every Friday to attend the picture sales at Christie's and on Wednesdays I went to Sotheby's. The sales were quiet affairs in those days, attended mainly by dealers. A tiny girl of 18 bidding for anything that started at one pound must have made quite an impression on the old dealers and it was not long before I made friends. They bought me coffee and taught me how to mark my catalogue, how to bid, what the 'ring' was up to. When I managed to buy anything, they helped me to sell on at a profit.

With my £2.10 shillings pocket money I started my collection of unfashionable 20th century English pictures; the ones that survived my impoverished years are still hanging in the White Sitting Room at Langar Hall.

I started buying pictures for my father who reimbursed me when I brought them home. I never asked him for a profit. I was happy to go back and buy again the following week. Among other treasures I remember a portrait of my mother's ancestor, Bishop Trelawny, by Kneller in its period frame; a charming contemporary copy of a group of children after Reynolds and a huge Oudry of domestic birds which I sold to Zwemmer in his bookshop in Charing Cross Road. This last sale led me to my first proper job in a modern picture gallery.

That summer I was cooking at Langar for the annual house party my parents held for the Trent Bridge Test match. I cooked for journalists and poets, generals and majors as well as famous old cricketers of the 1920s and '30s: even, on one occasion, Don Bradman.

Bill Crowe the gardener served at table and I joined the guests for coffee in the study after dinner. On this occasion my uncle, an artist, brought his friend Freddie Mayor to stay at Langar Hall. Freddie hated the country. Thinking I was the maid, he was amused that his county hosts should be so avant-garde as to invite their servant to join the party. He moved to sit next to me on the brown leather sofa. I knew exactly who he was since I had visited his gallery in Brook Street where he exhibited the most exciting modern French and British paintings and sculpture. Before the war, he had introduced Picasso, Braque, the cubists and all those classic French painters to London. I opened the conversation by telling him of my first sale to Mr Zwemmer. He was impressed: 'I've been trying to sell the old bugger a picture for years,' he said. 'Come and work for me in September.'

It did not occur to me that he was more than a little drunk and might forget his offer in the morning. I was over the moon. I was going back to London to work in a gallery off Bond Street. I was on my way! My elation was swiftly followed by a Big Family Row.

Working in an art gallery (with the exception perhaps of Agnews) was out of the question. And a modern art gallery, well that was what my father called 'arty tarty.' I let the subject drop but at the end of August I turned up at the Mayor gallery, very nervous but confident. I looked the part in high-heeled black patent leather court shoes and a neat new grey suit. Freddy had no recollection of offering me the job and I had to remind him who I was. He immediately sent me off to view Christie's (which was closed) while he telephoned my father. They arranged that Freddy would pay me £2 10 shillings a week to keep me out of trouble from Monday to Friday, 10am-5pm, with an hour off for lunch. My father would continue to pay for my lodgings.

The two years I spent at the Mayor gallery influenced the rest of my life. It was an exciting time when modern paintings were just starting to fetch serious money at auction. Freddy had some good clients and liked to pay record prices at sales for something he really wanted. This brought us great publicity and another excuse for party.

I viewed every modern picture sale, diligently marking my catalogue and reporting back. Artists, writers, actors, bankers, dukes, American art dealers, French gallery owners walked through the door, past my desk and waited for me to show them through to the Holy of Holies where Freddy was invariably asleep after a good lunch. I met Peggy Guggenheim, Peggy Ashcroft, Gregory Peck, David Niven, Richard Attenborough, Robert Morley, and most of the leading artists of the day: Duncan Grant, Augustus John, Max Ernst and those Cornish ones whose names I can't remember. I seldom recognised a celebrity and once asked Richard Attenborough how to spell his name.

On Sunday nights Freddy and his wife Pam often invited me to dinner at their Chelsea home, 50 Sydney Street. Pam was a very good cook. At first these dinners were rather intimidating but I soon enjoyed the company and, best of all, I discovered wine. Smooth old claret. It was years before I recognised that gloriously subtle taste again and when I did, I made sure to have a selection of old Bordeaux on the wine list.

'Arty tarty?' My father could have been right. London was at the dawn of the Permissive Society. Artists led the way. Eventually I found myself stuck with a good- looking boyfriend who actually wanted to marry me. It was time to move on.

When I was 21 my father gave me £500 to invest, plus £100 for not drinking spirits or smoking up to that time. I bought a second hand 1954 red MG TF and drove off with my school friend Coty, through France to Florence. We enrolled in a school to learn Italian. I found a nice pensione with a view onto San Lorenzo. Signora del Ponte with her lovely daughters lived in the family flat at the top of the stairs on the left; on the right the rooms were let to students. To get to our room we had to run the gauntlet of men who hung around the entrance laughing at their own rude remarks, which we did not understand. Men climbed up and down those stairs all afternoon and late into the night. Sadly we were not invited to the parties that the 'family' seemed to hold nearly every night.

My friend duly went to school while I spent my days in the museums and art galleries. To avoid the barrier of men at the door, I only went back to the lodgings at the end of the day when I had eaten as much pasta as I could afford in the restaurant down the road. Our room became a meeting place for the other lodgers. Outrageously flirtatious young men with a mission, they said, to teach us Italian. The first thing we learnt was that we were living across the landing from the best brothel in town.

Bottom pinchers stalked the Uffizi and it was impossible to sit down for a moment to contemplate pictures or panoramas without attracting the attention of the neighbourhood molesters. The charms of Michelangelo's David and the Boboli gardens faded. I was in no mood for Latin lovers and so, abandoning Coty and the car in Florence, I left to join Myles Hildyard in Athens.

A friend of my father's recommended him as a perfectly safe and dependable companion for me. I only knew Myles from a brief introduction at a cocktail party before I left England. He lived in a great Victorian House near Langar and I thought he was wonderful. Several years older than me, tall, intellectual, aristocratic and aloof, he did not suffer foolish remarks at all. He had a gallant war record, fighting from the first day to the last without killing anyone. He told me that the war was the happiest time of his life. Days by the sea when the sun was always shining. Myles was my hero, my Mr D'Arcy. He remains my best friend and I love him to this day.

Athens airport was under construction when I arrived a few hours late. The tannoy called my name to the information desk where a message was waiting for me: 'It's perfectly safe for girls to eat ice cream in Syntaganon Square. See you in the morning.'

My taxi drove through olive groves towards the city, the driver pointing out the Acropolis softly lit, just visible on the horizon. My room at the hotel was an empty dormitory of white painted iron beds on a rough wooden floor; my bathroom a row of basins and crouch lavatories in cubicles. Outside, Platia Syntaganon was lined with cafes spilling out into the square. I chose the nearest one, ordered an ice cream and watched the world go by. With the exception of a smiling waiter no one approached me. I was free.

I followed Myles round Athens, Hydra. Delphi, Delos, Mykonos, danced with sailors in cafes, partied on yachts and enjoyed the hospitality of his sophisticated friends. In quiet moments he educated me with tales of Greek mythology, read aloud from the

Guide Bleu or played chess. When it was time for Myles to return to England I was bereft. When I complained that I did not want to return to Florence, he said: "Imogen, in this life you don't have to do anything you don't want to. It is more important to know what you want and do that." What an amazing new heresy! For a second I thought of the nuns and the catachism phase: 'The devil and all his works and pomps.' This must surely be a pomp. I stayed on in Greece for six months.

Greece in the late 1950s was emerging from the German occupation in the war and its own cruel civil war. It was unbelievably lovely. The clear light, the freshness of the air even in summer, the music, simple food and retsina. Every detail delighted me. I drove through the Peleponnese to the Mani with Charles Schoop and his boyfriend Sotiri in a red Mercedes with white-walled tyres. 'Partners', 'relationships', 'gay' and all that political correctness had mercifully not been invented. Sexuality was rarely discussed in public. Carlos explained that all men were fundamentally 'queer' and I believed him. Years later he complained that he had been a 'queer' all his life and he'd be buggered if he was going to be 'gay' now.

Children ran to welcome the car as we drove through villages. Greeks bearing gifts of melons and grapes approached to ask where we came from in faltering English, learned long ago in the US where they were proud to have worked in their youth. Coming from Nottingham, I was especially popular; 'Nottingham Forest' they cried with enthusiasm. They knew every detail of the team from watching football on television in the taverna.

When the car broke down we stayed in a cottage by a silver beach where olive trees grew in the sand. We swam out into the bay and drank fresh water from an underwater spring bubbling up through the salty sea. Sadly a rumour went around that we were Germans returning to find the gold we had hidden in the mountains. One morning when I was filling water cans at the well, a shower of stones fell around me, I was not hurt but I was quickly dragged away to safety by a friendly Greek lady dressed all in black. Sotiri laughed when he heard the tale and explained that stoning was quite usual in the villages. Charles decided we could not stay in that paradise.

Twice a week we took the boat to Kalamata to buy the necessary parts for the car. Fishermen turned mechanics and a few days later we were back on the road heading for Koroni. This pretty little town, built around a square shaded by plane trees, with its back to the sea, faced the great ruined walls of a Venetian fort. A long sandy beach stretched away on the other side.

After a few weeks of renting a rat-infested house with an outside lime toilet 'hole', Charles bought a plot of land inside the fort overlooking the sea and set up camp. He employed a gang of local builders who carried everything up the steep, narrow incline from the village. Days were spent choosing marble, tiles and huge terracotta olive jars for the garden. Then, just as the roof was ready to go on, we were arrested. Planning permission was not complete.

Prison was hot, uncomfortable and boring. I just sat there with nothing to do, nothing to read until Charles agreed to stop building. The house was eventually finished by planting trees that grew up to fill the gaps and form a roof. I saw it years later when sweet-smelling oleanders flowered from the ceiling. I was sad when Charles abandoned that first house to build a palace further up the beach.

Eventually I left for home, taking the boat up the Adriatic coast to Venice. The old boy friend met me at the docks wearing a blazer. That blazer was the end. He had collected the MG from Florence and drove me back through Germany. I was ill most of the way. We parted in London never to meet again.

The next time I ran away from a highly unsuitable lover (who never asked me to marry him), I went to Paris. Freddy Mayor said it was time I learnt to speak French. He gave me some good contacts and checked up on my progress when he was in Paris on business. I accompanied him round the galleries during the day and in the evening he took me to Engains Les Bains to gamble. I stood behind his chair while he lost money at chemin de fer. I diligently went to school at the Alliance Françoise in the Boulevard Raspail, supplementing my income by giving English lessons. 'Uncle' Mouradian gave me a part time job in his Gallery Mouradian Vallaton, 41 Rue De Seine.

'Uncle' Mouradian came to Paris from Manchester for a brief holiday before the war, fell ill with measles and never left. I loved his stories of life in Paris in the 1930s, how he 'discovered' Modigliani and the terrors of hiding from the Nazis during the occupation of Paris.

His tiny gallery was a meeting place for artists and collectors, French and English. He lived with his wife and most of her family in a large airless flat in the 16eme where the walls were papered with paintings by Max Ernst, Modigliani, Roualt and Soutine. It was the most amazing private collection I was privileged to see.

'Uncle' was uncritical, supportive, reassuring. He was the key to those two years of my Bohemian life in Paris. When the Algerian crisis brought tanks onto the streets and the British were advised to go home, I went to him for advice.

"Stuff and nonsense," he said. "Do you think they are interested in you?"

So I continued dashing around Paris in the red MG sports car, going from pupil to pupil teaching English to suppliment my income, watching for the expected parachutes to descend and keeping more or less to the curfew. I learnt the delight of good food, simply cooked; the easy pleasure of wine and long heated discussions with friends in cafes. This was the start of a lifetime's love of the French and, if I have any regrets, it could be that I did not, as I intended, return.

I went instead to work at the Grosvenor gallery in London. Eric Estoric, whose fine collection of Italian art at the Tate gallery I had not appreciated, offered me more money than I could refuse and I fell for the temptation. This gallery was into serious selling. Art had become hard currency. The easy times when Bond street dealers did most of their 'work' in the Grosvenor Arms were over.

I had a flat in Chelsea and swapped the MG for a new white TR4. Then I met and fell in love with Andrew Skirving. We were married three months later. Andrew was quite unlike my usual affairs. He was, and still is, the kindest, most considerate quiet man. He looked after me through the cold foggy winter of 1962/3. When paraffin ran out in the Kings Road, Andrew brought cans of it from his home in the Cotswolds. It was so nice to get back to a warm flat after work. Even more impressive: his car was faster than mine. He had not one but two Allards, one with a bonnet tied by a leather strap.

We were married at the Roman Catholic church in Chelsea followed by an afternoon reception at the new Carlton Towers Hotel off Sloane Street. I still regret that I was not married in Langar Church. That ridiculous ban on Catholics still stood and so, with my mother in hospital too ill to cope, I organised my own wedding in a rather haphazard way.

Andrew and I moved to Nottingham where we lived at 14 Cavendish Crescent, The Park. He and my father opened a picture gallery in Byard Lane. It was the sister gallery of the Bonfiglioli gallery in the Turl, Oxford. Kyril Bonfiglioli was a colourful character, the inspiration for the *Lovejoy* television series and the author of the Mordecai books: *Don't Point That Thing At Me*.

We bought and sold English 19th & 20th century oil paintings and watercolours which, after modern art, I found rather dull. I did not appreciate them at the time, which I regret. The large brown oil painting of the chapel of Haddon Hall, painted by Neiman in 1836, which hangs in the study at Langar Hall is among the very few we saved for ourselves.

Our daughter Louise was born in 1964. When we moved to Langar she went to the village school. Five years later we had another daughter, Muriel, named after my paternal grandmother. This enchanting little girl died suddenly at the aged of 18 months. The worst thing that can happen to anyone is to lose a child. After that nothing is daunting any more.

Walking from the house to her funeral in Langar church, I stopped to pick a rose. As I took the flower I made a vow to lead two lives instead of one, so that her short life would not be wasted.

From that moment my life has been led in directions that I could not possibly have imagined.

First, I became obsessed with a quest for knowledge of the spiritual side of life. Through yoga I discovered meditation and, inspired by the Beatles' Maharishi Yogi, I practised transcendental meditation for years. I discovered spiritual healing through the Harry Edwards Spiritual Healing Sanctuary which, 30 years later, I still contact when supernatural help is needed. I attended seminars on alternative medicine, health and healing and every kind of esoteric idea that took my fancy until I realised it was time to get on with my life. Only lack of funds prevented me from going off to India in search of a guru.

Years later I persuaded my daughter Louise, who escaped to live in India, to learn yoga so that one day she could come home to teach it. Reluctantly she agreed. But when she fell in love with her Yoga Master and came home with a baby and no qualification, I was far from pleased!

While my personal spiritual quest continued, I buried my grief by involving myself in local politics. I fought two elections to represent the local villages on Rushcliffe Borough Council; it became my mission to protect our vernacular architecture at a time when too many charming old villages and buildings were threatened with destruction. On the Council for the Protection of Rural England I fought to 'save' the countryside and with CND, I campaigned against nuclear weapons and the rest.

Andrew threatened divorce when I was invited to become a magistrate, so I enrolled secretly. But after a few weeks, he recognised my face in a photograph of new magistrates in the local paper. By this time, resigned and neglected, he forgave me again and I served for ten years on the bench in Nottingham. That invaluable experience brought me back to the hard realities of life and set me back on track.

In my spare time, I gardened passionately, restored oil paintings (rather well) to make some money and kept my interest in cooking. All this and my previous experience of food, art and people turned out to be great fundamental training for the hospitality business.

CHAPTER FOUR

Getting Started

When my father died in 1983, Langar Hall was crumbling and money was short. I wanted to sell up but first I needed £1,000 to renovate the house before putting it on the market. Offering dinner, bed and breakfast to American tourists seemed a good idea to get the money and so, quite unintentionally, I began to turn my home into a hotel and restaurant.

The usual way to start up in the hotel business is with money, backing partners, business plans and builders, interior designers and staff. I didn't have that option. If I had, I would probably have gone bust in the recession of the 1990s that closed a lot of country house hotels. With a largish house and no money, my immediate goal was to make a living, at least decorate the outside of the house and then sell it.

One morning, sitting at my kitchen table over breakfast, an article in the financial pages of the *Guardian* caught my attention. Strange because I never read the financial or sports pages of any newspaper.

'How to live in the way you would like to become accustomed' was the heading that attracted me. It named all the agencies that dealt with overseas visitors who might like the experience of staying in an Englishman's home rather than hotels or Bed & Breakfast houses.

Organising tours to historic houses was my only experience of tourism. Perhaps groups of Americans would come to stay and this could bring the money I needed to paint up the house in preparation for the sale.

At that time we could not afford to go on living in the house and the sale seemed inevitable. I was planning to move to France to set up a B&B for British visitors close to a three-star Michelin Restaurant, although I doubt I discussed this with my long-suffering husband Andrew who might not have agreed.

Anyway, I telephoned all those agencies. They were not encouraging. Nottinghamshire? Where is that? Northamptonshire? No, Sorry you are not in a part of England that attracts tourists.

The following day the *Nottingham Evening Post* printed an article on tourism. So, clutching the newspaper cutting, I rushed off to see the bank manager to tell him about my brilliant idea and asked to borrow as much money as I could in order to put in the first necessary bathroom.

No such luck! He glanced at the article, smiled condescendingly and told me that he was leaving soon to take over a hotel in Devon and, knowing what was involved, he politely refused the loan on the grounds that Langar Hall and I were 'high risk'.

I never heard what happened to the bank manager and his hotel but the magnificent old Midland Bank building in Victoria Street, Nottingham, with its mahogany counters and high ornate ceilings, is now a boutique named FCUK. I pass it from time to time, smirking with the satisfying pleasure of 'I told you so'.

Although my husband, Andrew, was less than enthusiastic about my latest project he came to the rescue and lent me £6,000 to install the first bathroom. It was finished on the morning of my father's funeral. Just as the first mourners arrived, the builders came down the stairs carrying their ladders and tools. The first step was completed.

Now I had two letting bedrooms sharing a bathroom, one with twin beds, the other a four poster. I had new mattresses, two sets of new sheets and towels but no guests. I rang the Tourist Board at Lincoln. They sent two men to inspect. Suddenly I saw the house through their eyes, in need of more than just a coat of paint, and I was sad and a little embarrassed. I can see those gentlemen now, sitting on the sofa in the white sitting room, talking between themselves.

"This could make a nice small Country House hotel."

"Yes, but she has no experience and no funding. She would never manage."

I pretended I had not heard and silently vowed to prove them wrong.

Although they were not encouraging they kindly suggested that I contact Wolseley Lodges which turned out to be ideally suited for me to make a start.

Years later, one of the men returned with the Duke of Gloucester on some Royal engagement in the area. He remembered the first visit and was delighted to find Langar transformed and said he was pleased to 'eat his words'.

Wolseley Lodges was an organisation run from Norfolk by Proctor and Mary Naylor. It was a new marketing concept to encourage overseas and British tourists to stay in English homes instead of hotels or B&Bs. Langar Hall was their first 'house' north of Cambridge and we entered the book as No. 13. My lucky number.

> Bed and Breakfast £12.50 per person. Dinner £7.50. An honesty bar and bottles of quite good wine priced either £5 or £7 a bottle. Open Easter to October 1st.

I waited for the hoards to arrive. Only the fish man and the fruit and veg van came up the drive. The telephone did not ring.

Then one morning a big Geordie called Bob, overloaded with charm and persuasion, dropped in from the parachute school on Langar airfield. He wanted to book in a 'girl from work' who had agreed to do a 'jump' to promote his firm and he wanted to book her into what he thought was a nice hotel.

She was my first guest and her name was Mrs Rich. Another good omen. She lost her way, arriving late, too tired and frightened to eat the supper I had so carefully prepared. She did not want to do the parachute fall at all and was quite put out to find herself staying in a family home when she had been led to expect a luxury hotel.

The next morning a parade of hot air balloons drifted over the house. I took a tray of tea to her room and opened the curtains to show her, but she was too nervous to wonder at them and I was relieved when Bob came to collect her for the parachute ordeal.

When they returned in the evening, Mrs Rich was transformed. Exhilarated, happy, laughing and rightly proud of herself for being alive and well after jumping into the sky. I was so impressed that I allowed Big Bob to talk me into doing a 'jump' myself. Three weeks later, with a group of brave friends, we jumped for the National Trust, raising £3,000 for Kinder Scout in Derbyshire and Fountains Abbey in Yorkshire. After that experience, when I 'fell' out of the plane 2,000ft above Langar, the most frightening situations pale into insignificance.

Parachutists were some of my first customers; they had 'special rates' and I treated them with utmost sympathy.

Friends sent me my next 'paying guest,' a charming lady from America, the daughter of a famous portrait painter and widow of an early American aviator and aeroplane manufacturer. She was returning to trace a tour of England that she made many years ago with her husband. I took her to Chatsworth, Haddon and Hardwick Hall all in one long exhausting day.

By co-incidence she was a childhood friend of my next guest

from the States called Barbara Ford from Detroit. A large lady with Louis Vuitton luggage. When she told me that her father had collected delphiniums I guessed, rightly, that she was the daughter of Henry Ford.

Barbara insisted on taking her washing to the local laundrette because I did not have a spin dryer. My attempt at drying her vest in the fan oven was not a great success. She talked about the other places she had stayed on her way round England and reassured me that I was offering the most important things: a warm welcome, a comfortable bed and edible food.

Each guest was the most important person in my world. I used my best Skirving crested dinner service and Andrew's family silver for the guests until one morning at breakfast I noticed a gentleman inspecting the silver marks on his fork.

"Good heavens!" he exclaimed. "This is the first time I have eaten eggs and bacon with George III silver."

It was news to me too! After that I invested in a canteen of silver plate and some cheap white china 'seconds'.

That first year, the business hardly made an impact on our family life. It all seemed like a nice distraction and provided a bit of ready cash for shopping. But I needed to earn more than 'pocket money' so I joined some other agencies and attempted my first steps in marketing.

Elizabeth Grundy published *Staying off the Beaten Track*, a popular guide which sold in bookshops. This provided a steady flow of customers, mainly British, retired and looking for a good value weekend break. I liked Elizabeth as soon as I met her. She was a large, indomitable lady who I found refreshingly forthright and extremely funny. She inspected all 'her houses' herself, writing the entries and imposing punitive room rates which most of us tended to overlook.

One evening she arrived in a terrible state, having fallen off Hadrian's Wall earlier in the day. It was the time of the Libyan crisis. A couple of BBC news cameramen were staying and a young man in advertising. Guests dined together at one table so Elizabeth joined these 'lefties' for dinner. The conversation turned to war, which the young men were very much against. A pause in the conversation brought Miss Grundy to her feet. She gave them a good lecture on the importance of making a stand. A fierce argument followed and carried on well into the night.

I used to join the guests for a pre-dinner drink, tell them what was on the menu, and probably change it once I was back in the kitchen. Call them to table, serve the courses, clear and join them at the table for a few minutes if the conversation was interesting.

On another occasion a Romanian Countess, Ilsa Von Berekhousey, came to stay with her son Scarlet (named after O'Hara, not the Pimpernel). As I showed him his room he enquired about the dress code for dinner. I told that we did not have one and he could wear anything he felt comfortable with.

His mother and the other guests were gathered in the white sitting room for pre dinner drinks when he made his entrance. Scarlet was six feet three inches tall, well polished high heeled platform boots made him seem a towering seven feet tall. His long black hair was oiled and tied at the back. He was elaborately dressed in a silk Tudor style jacket with ruffled sleeves revealing a bare chest hung with jewellery. Black silk riding breeches, a tasteful handbag, make up, rings, ear rings and a stunning brooch made a spectacular effect.

There was a moment's stunned silence. I decided this was the time to break my rule and join the guests at the dinner table, in between cooking the courses, just to ease the situation.

Scarlet turned out to be excellent company and despite my trepidation the dinner party was a great success. He told us entertaining stories of the jewellery he made for stage and screen and his passion for Marie Antoinette. He invited me to see his copies of her jewellery, an amazing collection that he kept in a museum at his house in Hampstead. I learnt never to judge by appearances however startling. Thank goodness we have separate tables in the dining room now, although I enjoyed those lively evenings when guests and strangers had no option than to dine together.

Guest-Accom, a modest little publication which men on business round the country kept in their car, brought the mid-week clientele. Men, and a few women, who were glad to find a home from home and stayed on a regular basis. They seemed to run the place themselves, were generous with their advice, monitored the 'honesty bar,' corrected the bills and helped me with every kind of problem.

When I announced that I was going to Turkey on holiday in October and Langar would be closed for two weeks they pleaded with me to let them stay. They would, they promised, look after themselves and, as Andrew was still around to supervise, I agreed.

Leaving them with a ham and a Stilton cheese, I took the cash out of the china hen that served as a till, and went off to the sun. Two weeks later I came home to a rapturous welcome. The ham had turned green, the cheese had run out and the heating broken down.

Soon I was working round the clock, starting with breakfasts at 7am and finishing when the last customer went to bed and everything was cleared, cleaned and ready for the morning.

My daughter Louise came home from London to help me. She worked all hours for days on end. It was hard for her because she did not enjoy it and missed her friends and the social life that I soon found everyone in the catering industry has to sacrifice.

When she could not bear the daily grind any longer she booked a ticket to India and only returned in the summer to escape the monsoon.

I used to get very cross when she spoke of India as 'home'. How could anywhere be home but Langar, England?

Now she is happily married to an Indian yoga teacher and has two adorable children. They live and work in the Himalayas and migrate to Goa in the winter months. I spend every January with them there and I absolutely love it as my second home. Five weeks living the hippie life repairs the wear and tear of Christmas and builds me up ready to work for the rest of the year.

CHAPTER FIVE

Andrew

My husband Andrew, a most private person, suffered terribly from the constant flow of strangers continually in his house and he soon moved out too. Any other husband would have gone off and divorced me, which would have meant losing the house. Instead, Andrew moved out when the house became intolerably full of people and the last vestiges of his privacy were threatened. He patiently saw me through the first turbulent years without a word of criticism and continued to take care of the fabric of the house while at the same time creating a home for our daughter - and provided a much-needed bolt-hole for me to escape some of the self-inflicted horrors back at Langar Hall

Before he left he kept the study for himself. Pictures were stacked feet deep against the walls, books piled on the floor and boxes of every kind of bric-à-brac and small antiques made it impossible for me to use the room which became his last refuge. I even let our bedroom and moved to the little churchyard room where he sat sadly alone in the evenings while I beavered away downstairs in the kitchen.

He was rightly disapproving of the way my new venture was going but he neither remonstrated nor showed his anger. He wanted to escape, but although he looked at a couple of houses he did not have the capital to buy, nor the income to support a mortgage at that time. I was too preoccupied to help him and not understanding the depth of his suffering, resented that he would not or could not join in and help me.

Our friends were equally disapproving of this 'mad scheme'. My mother and family were dismissive, Andrew's parents were concerned and my daughter Louise disappeared to India. I was too busy to pay much attention to all the suffering I had unwittingly created. I was making some money and having fun with little time left in the day to think further than how I was going to cope with the next.

I was known in the county as 'rent a girl' - available to make up the numbers for hostesses when they had a spare man. Andrew hated going out socially and liked me to go off and tell him about it when I got home.

When an old friend and neighbour George Seymour invited me to a dinner party he was giving for the circuit judge, I reluctantly refused on the grounds that I had to stay at home that night and look after my paying guests.

So George was put out and, in an attempt to make me change my mind, he said:

"My dear Imogen, there are more things to life than money."

"Not when you have just spent too much money putting in a bathroom, there aren't," I replied. This struck a cord.

"Oh, I know! Only too well," he commiserated. "I've just done up a cottage on the estate. You know, the one opposite the church, on the edge of the park overlooking the cricket field." I could imagine it. "I thought I might retire there one day when Thrumpton gets too much for me."

George lived a sophisticated country landowner's life in a magnificent Jacobean house on the river Trent. I knew he would never retire to a cottage.

"If you're thinking of renting it in the meantime, I may have a tenant for you," I suggested. "Andrew is looking for somewhere to live, away from all the paying guests. Would you let it to him?"

George was delighted. He and Andrew enjoyed each other's company. They had become friends when George came to Langar to teach me to ride my motorcycle. And they met for tea when George gave me a lift home from the Shire Hall where we served on the Magistrates' Bench together.

Visions of George walking down the village street to call on his new neighbour, and Andrew watching village cricket or strolling in the park appealed to me and momentarily eased my guilt.

The lease was signed. Andrew and I went shopping like a young married couple, furnished the tiny cottage quite cosily and I almost wished I could move in with him. I thought he would be lonely after the joy of having his privacy had worn off and I was glad that Andrew was taking his beloved dog, Dudley, for company.

Dudley was an enchanting young border collie who herded the cats, put stray sheep back in the field and liked to take guests for a walk. He waited by the door for people to go out, then bouncing ahead, led them round the park.

On the day Andrew left, a guest asked if he could take Dudley for a walk along the lane, across the fields to Colston Bassett and back. Dudley trotted off beside him. They crossed the main road at the bottom of the drive and then, instead of taking the right fork which leads to the village, the guest took the left lane leading to a farm. The farm dogs rushed to guard their property and Dudley took fright and sped for home. He ran straight into a passing car and was killed outright. The car stopped and the shocked driver, followed by the distraught guest, came to break the news.

I left the guests waiting for dinner and dashed down the drive. I picked up dear Dudley's body and put it in the back of the car, covered with a rug. I felt I could not show my grief for fear of embarrassing the guests and I wanted to relieve the terrible situation for the man who had unwittingly caused the accident. So, I hid my emotions by serving dinner, making light of the situation as if these tragedies happened every day.

When Andrew returned to collect his dog before spending the first night in his new house, he was devastated. I had no time to comfort him before he drove away.

The next day, when the house was quiet, there was a little time to grieve. Andrew and I buried Dudley beneath the poplar trees and cried together, our tears expressing the loss of our beloved dog and so much more.

Years later Andrew bought a house in the fields between Langar and Colston Bassett, large enough for Louise and her family to stay when they are here during monsoon in July and August. It is a lovely house and provides a great escape for me these days.

Andrew still comes every day to check on me, the central heating and the trees he has planted. Today we call him the 'Curator' because of the way he still cares for the contents of the house, especially the pictures.

*

With loved ones far away and only my Pekinese for family, I was free to get on with the career I had so haphazardly created. I had no staff to start with. I thought that, with so few visitors, I didn't need any.

My old cleaning lady, Mrs Stevens, who worked for my mother before me, sang hymns as she thoroughly cleaned and polished the house from top to bottom on her well-organised rota. She made it clear that she disapproved of taking in 'paying guests' and did not include their bedrooms on her daily schedule. She would clean my room, do the downstairs and kitchen but never the guest bedrooms.

There were only two rooms the first year, and I found it a great chore to change the sheets and clean the bath. This is still the one job that I will not do and make certain never to be short of housekeepers to carry the sheets up and down stairs and, justly, take a pride in their work

Bill Crowe the old gardener had worked as a boy for my grandmother, accompanied my father to the war, and looked after me all my life. He thought 'taking in guests' was a great joke. "Wonder how long this will last?" he laughed.

Bill grew quantities of exquisite vegetables and soft fruit. The greenhouse was full of tomatoes and grapes in summer, houseplants and seedlings in the winter. His garden was immaculate. I was very spoilt and took the rewards of his seemingly effortless work for granted.

These good and loyal old retainers died before Langar Hall really got going and I was lost without them. Professional cleaning ladies and vegetable gardeners with that kind of experience and dedication are now extinct.

It was ten years before I found Rosie, a proper gardener and plants woman. Another Bill does a good job on the vegetables and procures limitless game from the Belvoir Castle estate and Jack Kent's mowing men keep the lawns and woodland paths immaculate. In the meantime, Bill Crowe's orderly vegetable garden went quickly wild and the garden and I suffered at the hands of a series of 'cowboys' claiming to be gardeners. They hacked trees and shrubs, broke the lawnmowers and stole power saws, hedge clippers and anything else they could sell at car boot sales.

A nervous little lady replaced Mrs Stevens. She dusted and hoovered in the week and a couple of local schoolgirls cheerfully did the rooms on weekends.

Then I employed Nigel. A stocky, dark young man who lived in the village, I had known him and his parents since he was a child. When he came out of prison and could not find a job he used to come round to see me and 'fix' my motorbike. When my husband was out in the car this Kawasaki 125, which I proudly learned to ride, was the most economic way for me to get around and I loved it.

Nigel started with odd jobs and grew into my 'Man Friday'. He did everything slowly with good humour. 'Repairs' and questionable car maintenance were his forte. He seldom finished a job, often disappeared but he kept me amused with his inaccurate command of language, especially Police jargon: "Draw the vehicle up to the kerb and I will alight onto the pavement," was the first phrase I encountered when I gave him a lift to Nottingham.

Although he only lived round the corner in Church Lane, Nigel turned up to work in a different car every day. Sometimes he arrived very early 'for breakfast' and other doubtful activities. He liked to hide my purse and cigarettes, then miraculously 'find' them, which he thought made him quite indispensable.

When he helped me service the bedrooms he insisted on cleaning the top of the door first. "That's where they look," hc insisted. Sometimes he came to work dressed in a disposable paper chemical warfare suit, complete with a hood that he wore, to the astonishment of lingering guests, when he laid the fire and brought in the coal.

Serving breakfast, "Fried eggs and bacon excellent," he would confirm, only to come back with scrambled eggs and tomato. Then he cleared the rubbish, mowed the lawn and went off to visit his partner-in-crime to buy and sell more second hand cars.

Nigel and his 'business partner' Philip were affectionately known by the police as 'Sooty and Sweep.' Nigel was his own boss. He enlisted for a Government enterprise scheme which gave grants to encourage people to start their own business. He called his business Aaron Services so as to appear first in the Yellow Pages. His other jobs became increasingly suspect.

After a few years, we had a visit from the taxman investigating Aaron Service's lack of tax returns. Suffering from the ridiculous illusion that I was somehow responsible for looking after the interests of my staff whether or not they cared for mine, I thought the best way out would be to put Nigel on our books for the work he did here. I missed the golden opportunity to dispense with this rascal and I lived to regret it

Nigel liked his position as my sole 'assistant' and when I employed a new member of staff, money and items always went missing and the suspicion naturally went on the most recent employee. The situation worsened when Aaron Services fell out with the car dealing fraternity, started a scrap metal business and 'cleared' everything metal that was 'lying around' including a cherished copper container from the greenhouse waiting to be planted with bulbs. That was too much! I summoned Nigel. Our meeting was loud with recriminations, threats and accusations. He returned a few hours later, naked except for his ghastly peach satin shorts, threw his bunch of keys on the table and stormed out.

Taking this as his resignation, I paid him a month's salary and wrote a nice letter, thanking him for his work and leaving him with the last of the second hand cars, which I had bought for his use. I did not see him again for a year and then we met in court where he was claiming unfair dismissal. He had worked for me for seven years and this was serious.

Mr Michael, an expert in tribunals, organised a pre-court hearing and he advised and instructed me. After five gruelling hours of aggressive cross-examination the charge was dismissed. Jan's detailed records and my personal diaries, which I kept daily at that time, proved there was no case to answer. Mr Michael's invaluable help saved us from costs in excess of £10,000 which, at that rocky period, would have liquidated the business. He refused to charge for his advice and he is still generous with his help whenever similar situations arise.

Nigel shook my hand without animosity. He was red in the face and close to tears. His latest hope of getting rich quick had failed. "Well, Mrs S," he said sadly, "I won't try that again. It hasn't proved remunerative." We remain on friendly but distant speaking terms. A few years later, when Nigel moved to Bingham, Andrew bought his house. One Church Lane became the staff house and is known in the village as the French Embassy.

Paper and cash were never my strong point. My books, if you could call them that, were a mess. I was always tired and accounts were the last thing I wanted to cope with.

When the PAYE man, Mr Whittington, first paid us a visit and saw the mess, he kindly put me in touch with Janet Teather. Janet travelled round to farmers in the Vale of Belvoir doing their books and she was used to people like me. When she found I kept the cash in a china hen and saw my 'invoices' she laughed and started to put the two previous years accounts in order. Mr Whittington was pleased and the system she set then lasted through to computerisation.

As Langar Hall grew busier, I prayed for help. I marched round the park invoking the spirits of Langar and wrote to the Spiritual Healing Sanctuary at Shere for guidance. Eventually I put an advertisement in the Nottingham Evening Post hoping to attract a local lady who could cook breakfast, work from 7-10 in the morning and be pleased to earn £2.50 an hour.

The only candidate who turned up for an interview was Jan. She was looking to change her NHS job in the mental health department where she was in charge of the patients' pocket money. Her office had been moved from Saxondale to Nottingham and she missed the view. A view was something Langar Hall had in spades. Her cooking experience was limited to the Cubs annual summer camp. She said she was an Akela but I thought she said she was an archangel and I needed a heaven full of them. But there was no question of her coming to work before 7.45am, too late for my businessmen.

When she told me she started her career in the Post office at 14 and had worked on early computers I realised that this intelligent, pretty, bouncy woman was exactly who I needed to do the books and run the office.

From that day Jan took over the bookings, accounts, wages, paid bills, chased creditors, checked invoices, sorted out the bank, worked with the accountant, dealt with the VAT, the percentages, profits and losses. She kept detailed records of the hours worked, holidays due, accidents, fire practice and my spending. 'Nanny Jan' has looked after me and Langar Hall through thick and thin. Nothing gets past her. She has saved me from all the pitfalls that can, too easily, lead to ruin.

Jan had a friend, Jean, who took charge of the bedrooms, organising her own team of girls and the laundry. From the day she arrived, I never had to worry about servicing the rooms. Her son Darren came after school to wait at tables until he left university to earn proper money with computers in London.

Of course Jan and Jean had a friend who would love to cook the breakfast. And so Grace, a most attractive widow, arrived and cooked good breakfasts until she left to marry again, very happily.

Langar Hall was on its way.

CHAPTER SIX

A Question of Chefs

Anthony Bourdin in his book *Kitchen Confidential* said it all about chefs. His stories ring absolutely true. I enjoyed the book enormously and found it strangely comforting. It made me realise that I was not alone when, time after time, I employed chefs who when interviewed seemed to offer the skills and stability I needed but soon turned out to be self opinionated, manipulative rogues.

My first chef, Esteve was just 19 years old. He wanted, above all to play his guitar and sing in a rock band. He came to England from a Normandy village to work at Les Artistes Gourmands, the only good restaurant in Nottingham at that time. Eddie Keon, the owner, employed French staff who came primarily to learn English and gain some cooking experience.

One day Mr Keon telephoned to say he had a young chef who wanted to earn a bit of extra money and would I like to employ him to cook lunch on Sundays when his restaurant was closed? The last thing I wanted was to open on Sundays but I never say 'No' to an opportunity because you never know what it might lead to. This opportunity led a very long hard way.

At that time I did not know the difference between a commis chef, a head chef and I had never even heard of chef de partie and all those other titles that make up a 'kitchen brigade'. I was so naïve that I imagined Eddie Keon managed to cook in the kitchen and welcome his guests at the same time.

With my brothers (Left to right: Tony, Peter and Mark)

My father's boat, the 'Bawneen', in Ireland

*Langar Hall dining room and
the Edwards Room, 1954*

At the Gallery Mouradian, Paris 1961

'Uncle' Mouravian, Paris 1961

Andrew and I in 1963

The portrait of me in my wedding dress 1963
that now hangs above the staircase at Langar Hall

*Andrew and I at Langar Hall with Louise
and baby Muriel, 1971*

Pascal and I in the kitchen at Langar Hall

Toby

Crispin and Toby and I

Crispin performing at Christmas

I loved cooking and assumed, wrongly, that all chefs must love cooking otherwise why would they choose it as their career? So when I interviewed Esteve I failed to ask him if he had ever cooked a traditional English Sunday lunch. He hadn't.

Esteve was a dark, sulky charmer who made the best onion tart I have ever tasted but otherwise his repertoire was limited. He was passionately in love with a little blond waitress and he did not want to spend his Sundays in my kitchen at all.

For my part I did not understand the difference between cooking domestically, for family and friends and cooking dishes for a restaurant service when customers have a choice and sit down in stages over a period of time. It took me ages to understand this and many hours wasted in needless argument.

Finally Esteve and I compromised on a set menu without choice. The menu started with onion tart, followed by roast beef. For dessert he made 'Isle Flottant,' a kind of half-cooked meringue floating in a sea of crème Anglais, which I recognised as proper custard.

I set about sending flyers to advertise the project locally. The response was extremely good. Bookings flowed in.

Few restaurant chefs know how to roast a joint of meat and Esteve was not one of them. He would not or could not attempt Yorkshire pudding. He found my domestic kitchen a challenge, usually turned up late and once caused a riot when he forgot the roast potatoes.

With the help of young schoolgirls I carried the plates to and from the dining room unaware that the chef had no idea of which table was ready for the next course as I failed to tell him which table I had just cleared. I could not understand why it took such a long time to serve lunch and I was even more puzzled when I found Esteve playing his guitar by the cooker instead of plating up the beef for the waiting tables.

There was an opening for a pleasant Sunday lunch venue in this area and many people came out of curiosity, expecting to find a reasonably decent meal in a lovely house. They went away disappointed, in astonished disbelief. No one was rude or unpleasant, they thanked me politely as they paid their bill. No one complained or asked for a refund, but they never came back and soon the bookings dwindled.

The Sunday lunch venture was an unqualified failure and it was years before our reputation recovered.

When Esteve's 'stage' at Les Artistes Gourmands came to an end he asked if I would give him a full time job and employ his friend, Pascal, as a waiter.

I was finding it difficult to juggle my time and needed to pay some attention to the sadly neglected garden. So despite the Sunday lunch fiasco, I agreed. Esteve could be trusted to cook nice French food for the hotel guests and French staff, I thought, would add certain panache to Langar Hall.

A flat was made for them in the wing of the house. It was not long before the girl friend moved in and then every kind of trouble started.

Chefs need to be kept busy and a hotel with just five bedrooms did not produce enough work for Esteve and Pascal. They soon persuaded me to open for dinner for customers outside the hotel.

Out went the flyers again and again the response was encouraging.

We devised a limited £15 three-course menu written, by Pascal, in French. The food was not too bad, sometimes quite nice but the standard was never consistent so it was not long before I lost even the good will of the hotel guests.

Our liquor licence only covered guests staying in the hotel so restaurant customers were invited to bring their own wine. This was a big draw, especially as I was under the false impression that

I could not charge Corkage. Parties went on until the early hours getting very drunk on gallons of their own 'plonk' When all the staff had gone home I frequently ended up in the kitchen making bacon butties, threading the revellers into taxis and clearing away just in time to lay up breakfast.

My cosy domestic kitchen was moved to the big old kitchen at the back of the house and fitted with second hand catering stoves, steel tables and a grill too high for me to use safely. I have horrid memories of spring lamb chops fried to cardboard and partridge thrown in the bin as 'English vermin.' I stormed and remonstrated. Why did I put up with all this nonsense? I still can't imagine. But worse was to come.

I had no conception of a restaurant and I wasn't really interested. I was determined to run Langar Hall on my own ideals of hospitality and this brought a lot of trouble both for myself and the young Frenchmen.

Esteve, verging on breakdown, called in his friend Franc. Franc walked out of his job at Les Artistes Gourmands to take over the kitchen. He saw at once that I was not *sérieuse* and I spotted that he was a seriously good chef.

Esteve and Pascal now had a head chef to direct him. The food and service was transformed. It takes just two weeks to make or break a restaurant and Franc certainly made the beginnings of the restaurant at Langar Hall.

I also learnt the danger of employing anyone who walks out of a previous job without giving notice.

Franc came from Vichy. He was incredibly thin, alarmingly pale and passionate about food. His food, and anything else, he dismissed as 'sheet' and would never follow a recipe or try anything I suggested. To make light of this difficult character I referred to him affectionately as Frankenstein and avoided his company during the day while he worked silently with immaculate orderliness.

He showed his disapproval by denying me food or access to food. I started snacking and grew fat. He would not cook for my friends or any one else he felt was 'taking advantage' and he certainly would not do beef well done or bend to please a resident customer who only wanted baked beans for their supper. He made mouth-watering desserts, the best scallop mousse ever and, under his management, the restaurant really 'took off'.

When we were both happy, after dinner service and customers' compliments, we met for a few moments of friendship. These occasions usually ended with fierce arguments, often lasting into the early hours. He bore no resentment and I knew that a lot of his complaints were justified. He tried to explain to me that a good kitchen porter or 'plongeur' was the foundation of a smooth running kitchen. I said I could not afford one. The argument was into its second day when an old man knocked at the kitchen door. Cap in hand, he politely enquired if there was a job going because, he explained apologetically, he had left his job as kitchen porter in a nearby pub because he did not like the new chef. He hobbled through to the office for a brief interview and started work that night.

Derek lived at Barnstone where he worked most of his life for the Cement Company. He was badly injured in an accident and in those days, receiving no compensation, had spent many years unemployed. Living alone with a menagerie of animals, growing vegetables, 'getting by', he was miserably lonely. Life in the kitchen at Langar suited him fine. He was a friend to me at a time when I was quite isolated and I loved him. After the chefs had left I no longer had to stay up until I had washed the last of the crockery and cleaned down the sinks. Instead I sat down with a cup of tea with Derek, smoking Park Drive and reminiscing about the old days in the village.

On several occasions he warned me: "There are two legged foxes at Langar Hall," but no matter how hard I tried to persuade him, he would never disclose the identity of those 'foxes' or tell me what he knew they had taken. He loved my Pekinese, Paris, and the two were inseparable. She used to ride home with him in his bicycle basket. I was jealous and not wanting to lose my beloved little dog, I gave Derek an adorable Pekinese puppy. He was very proud of it but he still loved Paris best.

One day, when Derek did not turn up to work, the message came that he had been rushed to hospital with a heart attack. I found him there looking unusually clean in a new pair of pyjamas. He was beside himself with worry over his animals and I promised to take care of them.

When Derek died a few days later. I was left with three dogs, including the Pekinese, two cats, ten ducks, a rabbit, four hens, a canary, a ferret and, worst of all, a Billy goat. We took all the dogs to Derek's funeral where they behaved very well, panting and dribbling at the back of the church in their sorrow.

I had no difficulty finding homes for all except that goat. I walked it back to Langar and tethered it by the grass hoping to encourage it to 'mow'. Instead it ate the young trees. It was neither pretty nor friendly and took a deal of looking after until a nice lady who just happened to be looking for a Billy goat, took him away in the back of her car.

After Derek died we had a series of unreliable young people who washed pots for money, but had I lost my late night companion.

A couple of years later, Franc decided to go back to France. He had had enough of the 'Theatre dinners' and the goings on that interfered with his cooking. He wanted his Michelin star and Langar was not the place to achieve it.

A week or more before he left we had a booking for a very important dinner. Mr Sidebotham, an important local businessman, needed a restaurant for a dinner he was hosting for a party of ten American businessmen, including the boss of a very large multinational company. He came with his wife to check the place to make sure that it was suitable to impress his important guest and fellow diners. They ordered their meal in advance to be certain that we could produce what he wanted for the dinner.

Lobster Thermidor to start; followed by whole grilled Dover sole. For dessert Tarte Tatin; and to complete the feast, our local Colston Bassett Stilton cheese.

With Franc in the kitchen, this was no problem and the dress rehearsal went smoothly. Franc and Mr Sidebotham went through the final menu in detail. Nothing was too much trouble.

Soon afterwards I realised there was one small problem with the plan. The date of the dinner was the day Franc had booked his ticket back to France. Could he possibly change it? No. Impossible! Esteve could take his place perfectly well.

Then two days before the day of the dinner, terrified of the responsibility of coping on his own, Esteve walked out.

I was on my own. I had never worked in that professional kitchen, the equipment was too high for me and I didn't know where to find anything. I was distraught over the lobster. I had never bought one, let alone cooked one. Well, I couldn't back out at this late stage so, I decided, I had no choice but to try and 'blagg' my way through.

Franc watched my mounting panic with amusement.

Was it at all possible to delay his departure for a few hours? No! Not to cook the meal but perhaps, if the lobsters were available at an early hour on the day of his departure, he would prepare them and show me how to serve them. But then he had to be off. I was pathetically grateful.

At four o'clock in the morning of the party I rushed off to the fish market. My luck was in. There were fresh fat Dover soles and a basket of live blue lobsters, their claws bound by elastic bands to stop them pinching. I felt terribly sorry for them. Franc kept his word and dropped them in a pot of boiling water. I just couldn't watch.

He prepared the lobsters, cooked the Mornay sauce and left them ready for me to put into a hot oven until they went golden brown on top.

The party arrived on time. Wearing my best silk dress, I greeted them at the door and mingled while the champagne was being served. Then casually I sashayed out of the room and, round the corner, sprinted for the kitchen.

The lobsters went out to the dining room looking good. But in my preoccupation with them I had given too little thought to the problem of grilling ten large juicy Dover soles. That grill was not designed for people under five feet tall. I needed a box to stand on. Then I had to get the heavy grill pan up and down from the flames as I wobbled on the makeshift stand.

Not for the first time, or the last, help was at hand. This time it was a regular hotel guest whom I called 'Yorkshire' because he came from those parts. As a 'regular' he knew life at Langar was never dull and he realised I was having one or two difficulties that evening. For the rest of dinner he ceased to be one of the guests and instead spent his evening helping me in the kitchen

He kept me going and made me laugh instead of cry. He handled the grill and those Dover soles were safely despatched to the dining room. I was able to slip out of my kitchen overalls, tweak my hair and make-up before sauntering into the dining room, once more the sophisticated hostess.

Mr Sidebotham was more than happy. He called me over and introduced me to Mr Big as 'the owner proprietor'. I felt I had never been so happy and after a few words, I walked slowly out of the room, breaking into a run and grabbing my overalls only when I reached the kitchen.

I really didn't want to face the oven again and wished I had persuaded them to have a cold dessert. But desserts are my forte and the Tarte Tatin turned out fine, dark with caramel, looking very edible with the ice cream just starting to melt by the side.

There was time too for the faithful 'Yorkshire' to eat his supper, enjoying the food which he'd helped to prepare. He was just finishing his meal in the servery when I went to the door to say goodbye. Mr Big insisted on complimenting the chef. Before I could stop him he strode through the servery on the way to the kitchen and found Yorkshire quietly eating his pudding. In the absence of anyone else he assumed 'Yorkshire' was the chef. Slapping him on the back he boomed:

"That was just great! Congratulations mon brave!"

I looked on in horror, convinced that 'Yorkshire's accent would give him and the secret of the meal away. But he just nodded and smiled appreciatively with, perhaps, just a hint of a Gallic shrug.

As the happy guests drove off in their chauffeur driven limousine, Franc and Esteve mysteriously appeared from the office where they had been hiding in anticipation of witnessing a dramatic disaster. I thought they were both in France and although very surprised to see them I was far too relieved and happy to be angry. So that crisis turned to success leaving me confident that I could get on to organise the kitchen again myself without constantly being held to ransom.

Well it did not turn out to be quite as easy as that. Dreadful times followed with a series of pretty dreadful chefs until I was brought to within weeks of bankruptcy.

It was time to do something about it. I needed an older chef with experience and I needed someone I could trust.

CHAPTER SEVEN

Toby

In August 1992 Stephen Clayton, known as the 'Colonel', returned to stay on the weekend of my birthday and took me out to dinner at Hambleton Hall to celebrate.

Their new head chef, Aaron Patterson, who was engaged to be married to our head waitress Clare, joined us for coffee. I seized the opportunity to ask if, by any chance, he had a chef 'up his sleeve' and explained how I desperately needed someone with experience to sort out my kitchen.

He told me that his best friend, Toby Garratt, who had helped him when he took over the Hambleton kitchen, had left because the pressure of work in a Michelin-starred place was not his style. He warned me that Toby was rather eccentric but he thought we would get on.

The interview was fixed for the following Sunday at 10.30am. By 10am I had finished cooking breakfast, taking care to leave the kitchen in order and determined to give the most professional interview to impress this highly respected chef. By half past eleven, when I thought they were not coming, I saw the group standing by the chest in the hall. Toby was dressed in a yellow T-shirt with blue dungarees. I was wearing a pink T-shirt with purple dungarees and I just went up to him, shook his hand and asked him: "When can you start?"

"I haven't got a car," he replied, but I was not going to be put off.

"You can borrow mine."

I started off by telling Toby my theory about the importance of a happy kitchen and how the chef's energy, while he was cooking, was transferred through the food to the customer. I had made a point of noticing this but no one took me seriously. Toby did not laugh; he agreed!

This was not turning out to be the interview I had so carefully planned. We talked for hours about the importance of using fresh, seasonal ingredients grown locally; my vision of a neighbourhood restaurant and the difficulties of getting over the pretentious Country House Hotel image of the 1980s. All the theories that had been brewing in my mind found an outlet and I found someone with even wilder theories than mine. We got along famously from the start.

Instead of a conventional CV, Toby produced some crumpled letters from his pocket. These were glowing references from Rick Stein at the Seafood Restaurant, Padstow; Tim Hart at Hambleton Hall, who had taken him back to work no less than five times; Tony Macintosh at the Groucho Club and 192 Kensington Park Road. I had no experience of the fashionable West London restaurant scene but I'd read glowing reviews of their modern British cooking.

When Toby was not working in those dungeon kitchens he had been organising free festivals and raves. His ambition was to buy a bus and make his fortune catering at festivals all over Europe.

When I offered him a salary of £12,000 a year, he laughed with derision but agreed to start the following weekend on condition he would only stay for five months. In that time he would set up the kitchen and find someone to take over. No problem!

After looking round the house he told me: "This place is perfect to do twenty lunches, thirty dinners."

"Impossible out here," I said.

"Mark my words," he insisted. "With clean plates and a healthy bank balance, we'll soon achieve it."

When I explained we were closed for lunch, limited dinners to 15 covers and did not open on Sundays, he was flabbergasted. The job started to look like a cushy number. He was not so happy when he saw the sadly unloved kitchen where the secondhand stoves and equipment were falling apart.

My acting head chef was on holiday at the time so I had the unenviable task of telling him that, in his absence, I had employed someone with more experience to take his place. I thought he would take his demotion badly and when he returned, I walked down to his lodgings to see him. I started off our little talk apologetically with "I have some bad news for you."

The colour drained from his face but, strangely enough, when I explained the situation he seemed relieved. Evidently he was expecting something much worse. However he still managed to make Toby's life in the kitchen as difficult as possible before walking out a month later.

Toby arrived in time to cook for a marquee wedding for 100 guests and was horrified to find we were serving Brake Bros. frozen pre-cooked food. He presented this as best he could, sending it out quickly, without enthusiasm. When it was all over, he asked to see the books.

After hours going through invoices with Jan he told her: "I'm sorry to say, but I think you are being robbed."

Toby changed the suppliers, replaced the frozen fillets of Argentinean beef with sirloins of local beef and started cooking very simple fresh dishes. He did the stock taking in the cellar in a morning instead of two days it had previously. He installed the computer system we still use to keep an account of wine: if one bottle goes unaccounted for, he and Jan have a witch-hunt.

I had been depressed by the apathy in the kitchen where the conversation between chefs was primarily about buying and selling cars. Toby talked about food all the time, threw out the car magazines, brought in cookery books and tried, without success, to inspire the young chefs with enthusiasm for their work.

Every morning he burst into the kitchen before the other chefs arrived. Soon there was a race as to who would get there first to accept the deliveries. Toby won and the other chefs, knowing their game was up, resigned. One even sent in his resignation by fax.

Under Toby's management, the numbers of diners in the restaurant picked up and when I found him alone in the kitchen, sometimes doing 50 covers, I went back into the kitchen to help.

I made the bread and the desserts, took the orders in the dining room, rushed back to the kitchen to plate them up and carry them back to the dining room. Working with Toby was enjoyable but hard, long hours and I got tired. We used to go to Sneinton market twice a week to buy our vegetables at three o'clock in the morning. One of us would go to bed to sleep while the other cooked breakfast and sleep later in the day.

Each day he reminded me, with a daily count down, of the number of days remaining to the time when the promised five months was up:

"Thirty six days and counting…" he would chant until the time to leave came sadly closer. Jan and I became rather depressed. We wondered how we could persuade him to stay.

After dinner service, Toby would sit down and talk to me. It was the only time since I started the business that anyone had talked to me as a friend. He talked about anything and everything other than work. He insisted that I recognise that I was a restaurateur and that restaurateurs enjoyed a wonderful social life. I did not believe it. The only life I wanted, apart from chatting up my favourite customers, was to go to bed to sleep.

In November I left Toby with some dubious 'help' and went to India to visit my daughter Louise. While I was away, Toby found a brilliant kitchen porter called Michael who washed pots shining clean, prepared vegetables, filleted fish, passed soups, butchered meat and cleaned the kitchen as it had never been cleaned before. Nothing was too much trouble for him; he often stayed into the early hours of the morning and was always smiling, never grumpy or cross.

This paragon of virtue, believe it or not, is the very same Michael who, as our Maître D' is as much part of the Langar Hall Restaurant as I am.

Michael had recently moved from London with his wife Carol. If you ask him where he comes from he often replies "Wales" or some other equally unlikely place. He was born and brought up in Ghana and came to England to join his parents in London when he was a teenager. Michael had the benefit of his grandparents' strong Christian upbringing. And it shows. His mother is an evangelistic preacher in East London and Michael is the most naturally Christian person it has been my privilege to know. He came with invaluable experience having managed the kitchen of a very large London hotel.

Big black Michael still comes to work late every evening. At ten minutes past six, after I have been watching the clock, he ambles in smiling his lovely smile, doing up his tie, murmuring about traffic. Sometimes I get cross; usually I pretend not to notice. I know that he will take charge of the dining room and I don't have to worry. For the first two years he made the kitchen a happy place at a time when it was very stressful indeed. Now he does the same for the restaurant.

When Toby first came, there was no money to replace mixers and other equipment broken by the previous chefs. When the cash flow perked up, we went to London on a shopping spree and I was taken to meet Dan Evans, who had offered to come to Langar when Toby went away.

Dan was taking a break while his kitchen at 192 Kensington Park Road was being refurbished and he thought he would like to spend time in the country. Although he had never worked in a kitchen entirely on his own, he volunteered to stand in while we found another permanent chef.

I was extremely flattered to have a chef of his standing, with a reputation for 'making' restaurants and who attracted rave reviews from the London food critics for his innovative food.

He arrived, three days late, on a large Duccati motorcycle, preceded by a car full of cookery books, at nine o'clock at night in the middle of a busy dinner service. As he walked in all the lights went out. I suspected this might be a warning from the Langar Spirits who were extremely active at that time. Looking back I think it was!

He took one look at Toby cooking by candlelight.

"I can't handle this. It's f****** driving me mad," he said and immediately went off to the pub.

By the time he returned it was too late for Toby to show him round the kitchen before leaving for Mexico. But I shall never forget Toby's parting words as he went out through the kitchen the door with a wicked smile on his face.

"Goodbye. Have Fun!"

When he returned, three weeks later, I had been through a crash course in food and wine, writing menus, and every possible drama that can take place in a restaurant.

Dan introduced me to his friend Hugo Arnold who wrote a food column for the London *Evening Standard*. He organised my wine list and published our bread recipe with a nice article about Langar Hall in the *Evening Standard*.

Dan's menu was simple, punctuated only by commas, no

superlatives or other nonsense that were in vogue at the time. But his dishes were new to Nottinghamshire; they needed explaining and selling. Dan often reduced Crispin and his waiter friends to tears, so they allowed me into the dining room to run through the menu. Ten years later, I still insist on doing this and I still enjoy describing the dishes.

Those few weeks with Dan were the only time in my life that I ever actually lost weight through stress. And it was worth it, although I would not wish to go through the experience again.

Dan understood how badly I wanted Toby to stay and suggested that if I offered him a partnership Toby might reconsider his plans.

I could hardly wait for Toby's return and as soon as he appeared, we sat down together by the cheese press with Polly the parrot looking on. The negotiations were not simply a matter of a profit-related bonus. Toby knew that I spent all the profit and more on 'building, maintenance and improvements.' What he needed was a very good reason to stay and work in his own place. He had had enough of being an employee and wanted a 5% share of the business. I agreed to that.

We resumed our exhausting work together. The quiet days became less frequent. We were always, in his jargon, 'going down big time' or 'on a Kamikaze run.' "Whatever" was his reply to all suggestions and questions, which I found difficult to handle. He burnt his arms on the stoves, slept when he wasn't working, never took a day off, had no social life and moved in to a tiny room at the back of the house to save the long journey to and from work.

He told me stories of his life at home on his father's farm near Melton Mowbray where he had 'trashed' the tractors, shot rabbits, run wild at school, played rather violent rugby, worked in the local Painted Lady night club and collected magic mushrooms from the fields around Rutland Water. I was fascinated. His grandmother introduced him to cooking, bridge teas, Sunday lunches and the good things in the life of a prosperous farmer's wife. He loved her and his grandfather and a punk girl called Lisa.

When Toby's grandmother came to call, driving an old Daimler, wearing twin set and pearls I was very surprised. When I returned the visit I was amazed to find her home quite delightful. Proper afternoon tea, Derby porcelain cups, Oriental rugs on polished wood floors and fabulous Queen Anne furniture.

"How on earth did Toby turn out like this?" I asked, pointing to the crumpled figure slouched smoking on the sofa, dropping his ash over her valuable rug.

"My dear!" she said, waving her arms in exasperation, "His mother, you know. We didn't get on. I wanted to send him to Oakham School but she would not allow it. He ran wild at that awful Melton Comprehensive and I lost control. When he worked in London it was even worse."

Toby's grandfather, one of the top freemasons in the county, a tall amused and distinguished Melton gentleman, adored his grandson. Toby visited his gradparents whenever he could get out of my kitchen and I think they were pleased that, at last, he had found somewhere he was happy to work with someone who appreciated his good nature and talent.

When Toby's grandfather died, Toby behaved very strangely. He didn't cry. He said he believed in re-incarnation and dashed off to London for the day. When he came back he swept out the woodshed. Unfortunately he dropped his cigarette end which smouldered and set fire to a pile of logs.

The *Test Match Special* team came back that evening to the excitement of fire engines and gave it a good plug on the radio next morning. Our new sous-chef (recruited by Dan), was so busy 'saving' his lover's caravan, which was in no danger, that he forgot his beloved new motor cycle, which melted. My new ride-on motor mower melted too. Toby was unconcerned. The sous-chef and his lover gave a week's notice.

Toby spent that night emptying his room. Everything he owned and half the kitchen was found, next morning, in the dustbin. I thought that a good sleep would make him better and calm him down. But he would not sleep and he got decidedly worse. The next day I took him to Nottingham to buy some suitable shoes and clothes for his grandfather's funeral; it was quite an ordeal. The shop assistants were politely bemused. His family banned him from attending anyway and as it turned out they were right.

That evening Toby distracted the terrified young chef by demonstrating how to make toast with a carving knife, otherwise he ignored the kitchen and the other staff were too busy to pay him much attention.

Jan and I did not know what to do or quite what was going on. But when Toby started darting round the house, dressed only in his grandfather's cashmere cardigan with a pink towel barely covering his vitals, to the amusement of some businessmen who were staying, we called the doctor.

The doctor called the Social Services; the social worker called the police. Toby went to bed to sleep.

The police arrived just as a performance of Chaucer's *The Wife's Tale* was under way in the restaurant. The dining room was packed with an audience of guests happily distracted by police cars and the ambulance passing the window. As the police entered, a group of actors, dressed as chickens, filed past the door. I was just in time to herd them into the Indian Room before they arrested the chickens. Two policemen, a young policewoman and two social workers drank cups of tea while we waited for the doctor to arrive and I tried to explain the situation. After what seemed like hours, I led the party upstairs. Two paramedics joined the group, which was now too large to fit into Toby's little bedroom.

Toby woke up and, peering out from under his duvet, gave the impression of being completely sane. The chief social worker timidly tried to coax him out of bed, into his coat and off to hospital, but he wouldn't move. Losing patience, I shouted at him and snatched away the duvet. He jumped up stark naked, pushing past the crowd, and invited them to have a look at my room before they judged which one of us was insane. I was deeply embarrassed! My room, across the passage, was the usual shambles of boxes, clothes, dogs and debris. I lost my cool and hit Toby with the menu I was clutching. He looked hurt and sadly pulled on his trousers, put on a smart cavalry twill overcoat, a jaunty cap and allowed himself to be led downstairs into the waiting ambulance.

I went with him in the ambulance to the hospital, taking the opportunity to lie down on the stretcher. I held his hand while he saw an army of terrorists shooting from the side of the road. He kept up a running commentary of this hallucinatory battle while the ambulance man booked a table for dinner in our restaurant for the following Saturday.

We had a long wait at the hospital. There were nurses around but no one spoke to us.

"I've had enough of this," said Toby. "We'll book ourselves into a good hotel."

Dragging me behind him, past the motionless guards, he made for the telephone. Alarm bells rang, big men rushed in, Toby did a neat demonstration of his judo kicks and ran off down the passage. Moments later he was dragged back, arms pinned behind him, by two burley security men. Jan, who had been waiting by locked doors, followed them and drove me home. We were very upset.

Two weeks later Toby, after winning an appeal, returned as if nothing had happened. It took him a few weeks to get over the prescribed drugs and others, and then he was back at work.

The doctors thought he was a manic-depressive, so I read up all about that and was duly sympathetic. The social worker and psychiatric doctor gave me wonderful support and the other staff were very understanding. They liked and respected Toby and never took advantage of the situation

I managed to find other fairly incompetent chefs through 'emergency chef' agencies and other sources to help. This was the start of very difficult time in the kitchen.

In the six years to 1998 I had Toby sectioned no less than four times, meaning that I applied for a legal order to have him placed in a mental institution on the grounds that he was a danger to himself and other people. When I eventually analysed the situations leading up to these destructive bouts of madness, I realised that they were all pre-meditated. On occasions when other chefs would walk out, Toby used his knowledge of drugs to take himself out.

He deliberately made himself mad when he could not cope with the stress. When my two grandchildren were born. I used to visit him in the psychiatric ward and Louise in the maternity ward at the same time. When his grandmother died, I did not take him shopping and he missed another family funeral. Another time, he could not stand working with a really nasty chef, who literally drove him mad.

When I realised this 'illness' was self-inflicted, I was extremely angry. Why did I put up with all this unnecessary chaos and destruction? Why didn't I give up and send Toby on his way as I always threatened to? Well, one good reason was that I couldn't afford to do that financially and, after all my experiences with chefs, I did not want to go back to running the kitchen without him. Even if he only worked a few months a year it was still worthwhile.

Anyway, Toby was not a drug addict. He was a drug user and he knew exactly how much to 'use' for the desired effect and he was never violent. When I weighed up the good against the bad, the good side usually came up stronger. Finally I managed by employing a proper brigade of seven or eight chefs which, with the support of Chris Ansell who came back to work for me three times, developed into a reliable team. They liked to work with Toby and they were not put out when he was 'off.'

Toby is assertive without being aggressive, inspires respect from chefs who want to work, and he can spot a bad employee long before I even notice. He loves to teach young chefs and has done so with great success. He is utterly loyal to me, and, rare in the catering world, he is scrupulously honest. I always feel indebted to him since he saved me from certain liquidation when he first came to Langar Hall. Despite all those dreadful times of destruction, I love him. My daughter Louise loves him too and we have taken him into our dysfunctional family.

If he was not such a good cook, I might not be so tolerant! But he is one of the few chefs I know who can cook a proper roast beef and Yorkshire pudding Sunday lunch and make slow roast belly of pork taste delicious with just the right crackling and no fat. When he is well he creates dishes that I really like, that sell well and make money. During one of his 'not working' periods, Spring crab gratin became Summer, Autumn and Winter crab gratin until he bounced back the following spring with another winner.

CHAPTER EIGHT

Crispin

One day in the spring of 1989 a customer asked me to do a party for the 200th Anniversary of the Bastille. He wanted his guests to come in period costume, a suitable menu from that era and after dinner entertainment. I agreed and went on holiday. I would think about it later. Think about it? Where to start?

As usual, I unloaded my worries on anyone who would listen until Caroline at the Bingham carpet shop assured me that her friend Crispin Harris would be just the person to take care of the whole evening. I was impressed that he was presently acting with the National Theatre Company and would be not be free until the end of the tour.

Crispin arrived to meet my customer for lunch in the garden on an exceedingly hot Sunday. Rotund and perspiring freely, he was not built for the sun but he sat patiently listening to the customer's ideas, making it plain that he was going to do 'his thing' anyway. Sweat pouring from his funny fat face, he moved lightly like a dancer, popping in and out of the kitchen where I was cooking lunch, keeping me in touch with the action. Searching through *Larousse Gastronomique* he came up with a menu that might have been served in Paris in 1789 when chefs lost their jobs with the aristocrats and set up take away food shops. That was the start of great French restaurants he told me and I was suitably impressed.

The following week Crispin had written a one-act play and was rehearsing a troop of 'resting' actors appropriately called The Scoundrels. The play was a clever adaptation of a short story by Thomas Hardy.

It was my first big party and I was more than apprehensive. July 14th was the most perfect summer's evening. The guests arrived elaborately dressed as aristocrats, guillotine ladies with their knitting, Scarlet Pimpernels, executioners. One group trotted up the drive in a horse and carriage. Everyone came determined to enjoy themselves and after champagne on the lawn I too began to enjoy myself..

We carried the first course, a large decorated sea bass, head high on a silver platter through the tables before serving it. This was followed by a stuffed wild boar's head, which I borrowed from a friend, also paraded to cheers and laughter. The real thing, when served, was disappointingly like pork. Boards of French cheeses, melting in the heat, were handed round and finally a pyramid of profiteroles roughly spun with sugar.

Then: "All quiet please for the play."

The ladies disappeared to the lavatory. The men got rowdy. Would they ever settle down to watch the play? Crispin, off stage, played the piano and sang in a weird alto voice. Roars of laughter and barracking. Then the actors came on and five minutes later everyone was captivated by a play. The performance lasted 40 minutes. It was magic and the whole evening was an unqualified success. I wanted more but the trouble was I did not have enough customers.

The following weekend, Crispin agreed to come to play the piano and sing before and during dinner. The first guest arrived before the waiter had finished laying the tables and, being less than politically correct telling him to get a move on, I caused the waiter to walk out.

When I took the customer his drink, I was still grumbling. He had witnessed the scene with some amusement and said: "Imogen, what you need here is a good old fashioned butler."

"Where on earth would I find one of those?" I retorted furiously and, turning to leave the room, I noticed the back of Crispin's bald head with its monk-like fringe at the back. There was that butler.

Crispin bought a tailcoat and a brocade waistcoat in a charity shop and quickly established himself as our 'Singing Butler'. He came in at six and took over the dining room. Word got round and soon we had a big enough following to put on Theatre dinners one Friday a month. Crispin wrote a variety of one-act plays for every occasion.

Tom Jaine, restaurant critic for the *Telegraph* and editor of *The Good Food Guide* wrote a lovely article. By chance, Paddy Burt, who reviewed hotels for the same paper, stayed on a night when Crispin's Alice in Wonderland was acted round the garden. His entrance down the fire escape dressed appropriately as the Red Queen delighted her and she wrote a rave review.

We went on to do two Summer Balls. Fire-eaters and jugglers and all kinds of extravagant entertainment and dress, not to mention donations to Romanian children, made disastrous losses. In the end of year accounts these were put down to 'marketing'.

Crispin always followed several other careers and attended regular auditions. Eventually he left to understudy Harry Secombe (and other parts) in Pickwick at the Chichester Theatre.

Without Crispin to organise them, The Scoundrels Players folded. By this time all our customers had seen the plays. With the arrival of Toby the food had improved so we kept busy without the entertainment.

Then a customer brought the 'Bella Voce' singers to entertain his guests at his 50th birthday party. I thought arias after dinner was a bad idea but they were even more magical than the plays. So 'Theatre' dinners became 'Opera' dinners which were equally, if not more successful. In time the group broke up when two of the original four singers won scholarships to the Guildhall School of Music and started their professional careers. Occasionally we still do these classical and light music concerts after dinner for private parties and when the group can get together on Christmas Eve their 'Carols' supper makes a perfect start to Christmas.

Then I met Patricia Knight Webb. She chooses a group of young actors freshly graduated from acting school and with her regular 'oldies' and excellent music, she marches them from Cornwall to Edinburgh playing in all weathers in all kinds of venues. Our Shakespeare in the garden is always on a Sunday in August.We have a buffet lunch or people bring their own elaborate picnics. Our first audience of twelve sat through *A Midsummer Night's Dream* in baking sun; the next year raindrops dripped from Shylock's nose. Recently, a record audience of 150 squeezed on to the croquet lawn where there is a natural stage. I think I make money selling cornettos at £1.50 and I look forward to the event as one of the best times of the year.

CHAPTER NINE

Barristers and Jockey Club

I never intended to turn Langar Hall into a conventional hotel. In my quest for credibility, this proved a great disadvantage. My experience of hotels was limited to student places in Paris in the 1950s or brief visits to the Sloane Court Hotel with my father. On occasions when I found myself in anything grand I felt uncomfortable, stifled by airless corridors and acres of fitted carpets. Not to mention the staff.

The only place I admired was Hambleton Hall on Rutland Water because of the food and service. It always seemed to me to be the epitome of perfection which I could never hope to achieve although I used its example for inspiration.

I wanted to keep the ambience of Langar as a private house, which I knew was its great attraction, and I was able to keep it that way until 1992 thanks to barristers and the Britannia Park case.

John Wright, an old acquaintance from the 1960s when Andrew and I used to be invited to his house in Derbyshire for smart, intellectual dinner parties, called to see me. He explained that he had a court case coming up and would like to stay with his two barristers for the duration. He explained that he was on legal aid and expected special rates. No problem. I understood this was a civil case and might last two weeks.

It was my good luck that the case lasted 18 months, making *The Guinness Book of Records* as the longest recorded fraud case in history.

Nigel Milnes QC, acting for the defendant, and his junior Stephen Clayton (known as the Colonel) were a delight to have to stay. We were soon taking bets as to how long the case would last, but nobody suspected that it would become a way of life. In all that time there was never a complaint or a cross word between us and the staff loved them. Even the chefs invented 'Tonight's Choice Menu' which changed each night so that their appetites would not be dulled by reading from the à la carte menu every night. We keep it on to this day and it is always good value.

The defendant was an extreme Christian Evangelist. He ran breakfast prayer meetings for businessmen, so he was often away staying with the 'County and Clergy.' The barristers' first breakfast with their client was such a shock to them that they were careful to avoid the Christian demonstrations of affection and prayer in the morning by coming down as late as possible

John, who was always up with the lark, was left to hang around the car park waiting to pounce on leaving guests in the hope of making a conversion. This was especially unpopular with the Jockey Club stewards who stayed when they were working at Southwell or Nottingham racecourse.

The first Jockey Club stewards who came to Langar ordered a bottle of Chilean red (very good value in those days) when they arrived at six o'clock in the evening. They carried on drinking the same wine as they talked into the early hours.

The next morning I questioned their wine tabs. Surely they could not have drunk six bottles of wine? I put four down on the bill.

"We definitely remember drinking six," said the two slightly hungover stewards. We settled for five.

After that we invented the 'Jockey Club bill' which we still use today. It simply states a total price for dinner bed and breakfast. Telephone and newspapers extra. It's popular with other guests who wish to avoid cross-questioning by their accounts department.

Eventually the senior Jockey Club officials from headquarters booked in to see what was going on. This, I think, was a contributory factor to a reorganisation in the racing world, sending stewards to carry out their duties at racecourses nearer their home.

With the barristers, and their colleagues from the Britannia Park case who often came to dinner, the Jockey Club and other regular visitors, Langar Hall became a kind of exclusive club.

There was Mr White who sang in a choir on weekends and liked to practise after dinner singing to Crispin's rather resentful accompaniment. 'Feathers' the attractive lady supervisor from John Lewis flirted with Mr White and Mr Green from Pedigree Petfoods

Standing by the parrot cage, talking to Polly (yes, we had a green Amazon parrot for 35 years) a man would invariably come up to ask: "Does the parrot talk?" Feathers never dined alone.

Langar Hall's name became synonymous with enjoyment, good food and good value amongst the London legal fraternity. There has seldom been a time since that we have not had at least one barrister staying and they still enjoy special barristers' rates. Criminal barristers, surgeons, doctors and other people who experience the dark side of human nature in their daily work are wonderful guests. Easily pleased, amusing, bon viveurs, they love to relax and enjoy the good things of life in contrast to the horrors they encounter during their working day.

For me this was perhaps the happiest era. My seven bedrooms, of very varied standards, were consistently full and by the end of the Britannia Park case I was confident that it was time to start transforming my guesthouse into a hotel. That is, a hotel that I would be happy to stay in myself.

But something was fundamentally wrong. As our turnover increased so our previous modest profits turned to loss.

It was another six months before I found the cause of the trouble.

CHAPTER TEN

Ghosts, guests and other spirits

We called the ghost 'Polty the Poltergeist' but I knew it was the spirit of my father, not come to haunt me but to warn me and protect the place he loved.

His family fortune was made from coal in the 19th century, and there was always an abundance of best quality Gedling coal piled on the fires that became so hot that the leather seats of the club fenders were burnt away. Down in the cellar, the Robin Hood self-stoking boiler burnt tons of 'Gedling singles' and the house would have been pleasantly heated had the radiators not been confined to the passages. The bedrooms were so cold that in winter, ice formed on the inside of the windows and the water in my mother's bathroom lavatory was frequently frozen in the morning.

In the early 1960s, when our neighbours switched to oil fired heating, my father insisted on using solid fuel on the grounds that he could trust a Nottinghamshire miner with his life but would never trust an Arab. So Bill Crowe the gardener riddled the boiler twice a day until he died and the mammoth boiler with its coal continued to take up precious space in part of the original 18th century wine cellar under the house.

Eventually, in the late 1980s, the coal boiler, by now of museum antiquity, broke down and had to be replaced. As I had recently fallen prey to Calor gas salesmen and their engineers were on site fitting a heating system in the wing of the house, I was persuaded to exchange the old boiler for a neat little gas-fired burner.

Andrew didn't like the idea. He wanted to save those big cast iron radiators that are now in fashion again, but I paid no attention. The gas men measured up and I awaited the estimates with their 'easy payments' or lease hire or whatever way of borrowing I could manoeuvre without asking the bank.

Then my father made his presence felt.

On three separate occasions, young male guests came down to breakfast and told me they had had a visitor in their room during the night. Each time they gave the same description of a man about five feet ten inches tall, stockily built and wearing a copper 'arthritis' bracelet. The young men assumed the intruder was a guest from another room but when 'he' tried to get into their bed, they shouted and he vanished 'into thin air.' I recognised the description as unmistakably my father. On each occasion the men happened to be staying in his old bedroom.

I took the hint and cancelled the gas. A new Robin Hood model boiler is still pumping away and every time I decide that I'd rather use the cellar for wine and call in the engineers to make the changes, someone always convinces me that I'd regret it. Coal heating is the most economical form of heating. The coal now comes from Poland or Uruguay (wherever that is?) and it is nothing like as good as the old Gedling singles. So I've put the plans on the 'back boiler' as they say, but I don't think my father would object if I was tempted to restore the old cellar.

*

Every evening as the clock struck six, my father would pour a cocktail. Gin and 'It' he called it. A glass of gin, a slice of lemon, no ice and such a tiny splash of Noilly Prat that it hardly dampened the rim of the glass. Gin and tonic as we drink it today would never do.

When the staff told me that a bottle of gin fell from its optic with such force that it flew over the bar and smashed on the floor, narrowly missing a frightened waitress, I thought at first that we needed a replacement optic. So I ordered a new one and checked that the next bottle of gin was securely fixed. A few evenings later I was standing with my back to the window, contemplating nothing in particular, when I saw the bottle of gin leave its optic at an angle, hitting the bar with terrific force, smashing a few feet away from me. That gin bottle was certainly looking for attention. I knew it was a warning but a warning of what?

The following Saturday, one of the barristers on the Britannia Park case, invited a friend from Derbyshire to join him for dinner and to stay the night. After a good meal, washed down with 1982 Chateau Palmer, the friend was offered a glass of the best brandy. He drank it slowly and, when offered another, refused, confiding to me that he thought the brandy had been watered down. I took a sip. Watered down? There was more water than brandy at £10 a shot. Now I knew what was going on.

The breakfast waiter at that time impressed me by coming in earlier than necessary 'to get a start on his jobs' long before the customers came down for breakfast. He had been systematically topping up empty bottles of brandy and no doubt other spirits, from a new bottle, watering down the bottle on the bar to cover his traces, while passing the rare brandy, undiluted, on to his partner in crime. As he did not drink himself, no one would suspect him.

The same thing went on with the wine. The staff said the cellar was haunted and that was where Polty hung out. When something went missing, down to the cellar they would go to ask Polty to retrieve the lost object and 'hey presto' that object would appear.

One day I was down there, standing still, wondering where to find a bottle when, out of the corner or my eye, I saw a bottle of wine slowly and carefully move out from the centre of the pyramid (we did not have wine racks then) and fall on to the stone floor without breaking.

Why hadn't I realised that the breakfast waiter could fill his black bin liner in the morning and the dinner waiters could take theirs 'out with the rubbish' in the evening? It was time to install a proper system of stock control

I copied the wine stock system from Hambleton Hall but it took eight months before I could get it up and running. There was always some excuse and it never occurred to me that, as everyone was involved in the scam, it was not in their interest to see it working. We lost tens of thousands of pounds this way before Toby arrived. He spotted this old catering game at once and had the system working within a week.

How could I have been so gullible? It makes me quite cross to remember what a fool I was and I am ashamed to have disturbed my poor father when he should have been resting in peace. It would not take supernatural powers to show me what is wrong today!

After my mother died there were no more activities from my father, so I assumed that she had taken him with her to a higher Roman Catholic heaven. The Langar situation climbed out of serious trouble and after that I had only dramas to cope with, no more stealing.

When a national newspaper wanted to interview the Scoundrels Theatre Company, Langar Hall was the obvious place for meeting. The actors congregated in the study where they talked to the journalist and a well-known photographer. Of course, they told some of their 'Polty' stories. After a while, they called me in to settle a disagreement about the ghost. I was reluctant, sensitive about something I considered personal and did not want to speak about it to strangers, especially the press. Walking in on a heated argument about the supernatural, I became annoyed with the photographer who was making a joke of it all and, as he left the study, he remarked:

"I hope your ghost won't damage my camera, it's got an expensive new lens."

"Our ghost would never harm anything," I replied as I followed him to the door.

To my horror, just as he reached the part of the stone flagged floor not covered by a rug, I saw his camera 'ripped' violently off his shoulder and fall with a crash on the stone floor. Luckily the lens was not damaged but the photographer was very shaken. He ran white-faced out of the door, oblivious of my apologies. Some months later I read that he had been killed in a car crash in Africa. I am sure that was nothing to do with Polty but no one laughed at his activities after that.

*

In 1991 builders were digging the foundations for the new wing at the Church end of the house when they came upon what seemed to be a mass grave of assorted skeletons. Work stopped for the Police, the local Health Authority and archaeologists to check for murder, disease and history. I was not best pleased by the delay but the skeletons were finally given a clean bill of health at around 300 years old.

I had been reading books about Lord Byron and, under his influence, I took a particularly beautiful skull in perfect condition to keep in Reception. I cleaned it up and put it by my desk, proudly showing it to any one who was interested. It even made a story and photograph in the *Nottingham Evening Post*. The other bones were left in a box with the intention of giving them a proper burial.

Crispin and I at one of our theatrical evenings at Langar Hall

Toby in the kitchen at Langar Hall

White Sitting Room (above) and the Study (below)

The elegant pillared Dining Room, formerly the grand entrance hall to Langar Hall, seats 30 at individual candlelit tables.

The Edwards Room (above), the principal bedroom of the house.
Bohemia (below) was once an artist's studio.

*The Cartland Room, a favourite of Dame Barbara Cartland,
and (below) Barristers, whose occupants were once involved
in the longest fraud case on record.*

The gardens at Langar Hall and (below),
Agnews, the garden chalet on the croquet lawn.

The 'Reluctant Restaurateur' outside Langar Hall after winning the 2003 Outstanding Achievement Award at the Nottingtam Restaurant Awards

After a rare night out, I returned home to a great commotion with the staff insisting that I remove my precious skull. The guests were all of a flutter because three glasses smashed simultaneously on a round table of seven. No one had touched them; they just snapped at the stem, spilling red wine over the white tablecloth. After the initial surprise, one of the ladies left the table to visit the toilet that backed onto the office where my skull was displayed. As she sat down, the lights went out and she heard the sound of more breaking glass. By now, really startled, she ran back to the dining room. When the lights came back on, there was no broken glass to be found in the toilet but a light bulb had come out of its socket and fallen without breaking onto the tiled floor.

I agreed to reunite the skull with the other bones and bury it with its companions in the churchyard. The builders made a very expensive coffin inscribed with the date and the vicar came to say prayers at the burial service. The service was held early one morning, well attended by a few barristers on their way to court, a couple of delivery men, the gang of builders and various staff. The only objection came from a fundamental Christian who was, at the time, on trial for fraud. He said it was the 'the Devil's work'.

The house was once attached to the Church and whenever we dig on the north side, bones are always found. This is the place, I am told, that was used for suicides and non-Christian burials but I prefer to identify the bones with the Civil War which raged around Langar in the 17th century. One misty October morning, the Langar troop of farmer's lads loyal to the King were on parade when they were ambushed by a posse of Roundheads from Colston Bassett and all were killed. It was probably their resting-place that I disturbed.

CHAPTER ELEVEN

Emergency and Dire Emergency

When the licensing magistrates, prompted by the fire officer, threw the book at my application for a restaurant liquor licence they gave me just six weeks to comply with their demands or else they would take my residents' licence away as well.

The fire officer's demands included a fire escape, partition walls, three fire doors, an electronic system with fire detectors on every ceiling, 20 expensive fire extinguishers and the necessity of opening up the house again to provide two staircases. Rather a tall order and after a few tears I telephoned the local builder, Theo Smith, and asked to borrow Arthur for six weeks. This was a good arrangement. Arthur and I had known each other from childhood and we got along famously.

I gritted my teeth while the pretty gothic window looking out onto the church was replaced by an ugly glass fire door, the pleasant proportions of the landing were wrecked by a partition wall and fire doors were fitted on the lower landing, blocking the light onto the stairs.

Downstairs, the fire consultant saved the handsome Georgian doors and arches. He came along to talk to the strictest fire officer in the area. They deliberated over tea and chocolate biscuits before retiring to the church to play the organ. By the time they returned the fire officer was my best friend and supporter.

Arthur and I set about opening up the wing of the house, making bedrooms and bathrooms as we went along by drawing the plans on the paper lining we found under the carpets. In order to save complicated plumbing we made the mistake of putting a bathroom in the corner of a bedroom and then dividing the room in two to make a family suite. But as very few families came to stay, I used the back room whenever there was none other available. Regular guests would plead: "Imogen, you must have somewhere! Put me in a cupboard."

For many years these rooms were known as Emergency and Dire Emergency.

Returning 'regulars' love to remind me of their experiences in these rooms and I cry with laughter.

I had no money to pay for the alterations and there was little point in asking the bank for a loan or Theo Smith for an estimate of costs. I just went ahead and hoped for the best. I had no option. The final bill came to £42,000. It so happened that on the death of my mother I inherited my share of the De Las Casas trust which her Spanish Cuban father had created for his grandchildren. The money came from his Havana estate that my father had sold after the war and invested the proceeds just before Castro took over.

My brothers had already sold their reversionary rights but I held on to mine. I didn't expect to receive more than £10,000. You can imagine how amazed I was when the cheque came through just before the builder's bill for exactly the same amount: £42,000. Is it surprising that I believe help comes from the Spirits of Langar?

*

Six weeks later I returned to court, confident that Langar Hall would be granted its restaurant liquor licence. To my dismay I was ruled out of court on the grounds that I was 'not a fit and proper person to hold a licence'. After serving years on the magistrate's bench, I thought this was a bit thick and I was absolutely furious. It was all a colossal misunderstanding, due to my carelessness. I had employed a blind solicitor from Bingham and for some reason he or his assistant had accidentally changed my application from a restaurant licence to a full licence. I did not spot the mistake until the case was well under way and, being confident in the witness box and at home in court, I attempted to explain my case. I interrupted my legal representative and argued with the magistrates. This was fatal and I was real trouble. On the steps of the courthouse my legal representative informed me that there was little hope of getting a licence now.

As soon as I got home I telephoned my old friend, George Atkin, 'godfather' of Nottingham Licensed Casinos and betting shops. I knew him from the days when he bought pictures from Andrew's gallery and ran the extremely popular Victoria Club. He had been to dine at Langar the previous night with a party of friends, bringing his own Champagne and cases of wine with him.

"Imogen, I'm tired of bringing my own drink," he complained. "When are you going to get your licence and a decent wine list?"

"Tomorrow," I replied with confidence. "I'm going to court and I've done all the work they wanted so the fire officer is pleased, the police happy, everything's in order."

"Well, if you have any trouble, let me know."

George must have been through many battles with the magistrates and he evidently had his doubts.

When I telephoned him later to tell him what had happened, he answered the telephone and offered his help without hesitation:

"I am going to telephone my solicitor John Pearce now. If he doesn't ring you back within ten minutes, get back to me."

John Pearce rang back immediately and came to call the following day. He went over every detail quietly and thoroughly, taking measurements and photographs of each room before going back to his office to fill in the application forms.

Six weeks later we met outside the courtroom.

"I want you to do something for me." He looked serious.

"Yes. Anything."

"I want you to promise not to say anything in court apart from 'yes' or 'no' to the questions I ask you."

"Of course." I was duly impressed. At that time, John Pearce was the one and only licensing solicitor that the Nottinghamshire magistrates respected. As I waited my turn I witnessed London solicitors, applying for their clients, turned down and almost all the other hopeful candidates failed to get their licence.

I kept quiet and to my utter joy and relief Langar Hall was granted a restaurant liquor licence with no trouble at all. The great advantage of being a restaurateur is that it's who you know that gets the job done.

CHAPTER TWELVE

Celebrity Guests

Celebrities have been a great asset to Langar Hall. Without exception, those who choose to stay at Langar have been unusually talented, intelligent, interesting, well-mannered and appreciative people who have helped and encouraged me. I guard their privacy fiercely and cherish them during their stay. Then, when they leave, I name-drop for all I'm worth because I love being associated with the rich and famous!

The Archbishop of Canterbury, Robert Runcie, was the first to come to stay. My old friend and neighbour, Tina Gibson, booked him in. Her daughter had worked for the Archbishop for several years so when she was married at Langar Church, he agreed to do the honours.

On the morning of the wedding the painters turned up to paint the windows on the outside of the house. As I had waited for months for them to do the job, I did not send them away. To my horror I noticed them putting a ladder up to the Archbishop's bedroom window so I rushed out.

"Stop, stop! The Archbishop of Canterbury is getting dressed in there," I shouted.

"I suppose you've got the Pope next door an' all," came the jaunty reply.

It took some persuasion to get them to move their ladder onto the other side of the house. Later in the day they were painting the bedroom window directly above the French windows leading out of the study into the churchyard garden. This was the way chosen for the Archbishop to leave the house on his way to church. Once more I had to ask the painters to move their ladder before Robert Runcie, in full white and gold regalia and carrying his staff, appeared in the doorway. The painters, mouths open in disbelief, stood respectfully aside. As he passed, the Archbishop asked if they would be so kind as to carry his mitre to the church door. The man not holding the ladder sprang forward to oblige. He is still talking about the day he carried the Archbishop of Canterbury's mitre!

The very next day the manager of Belvoir Castle came to see me. He was looking for a nice place for a very famous American television actor to stay.

"Langar Hall will be perfect," he said kindly. "Not ostentatious, quiet and private," he nodded to himself as he looked round the modest rooms.

"Please tell me who it is," I implored. "I need help. I never recognise anyone and it could be embarrassing." No comment. "I only watch Dallas, so it had better be J.R." He smiled.

The following week he brought Ken Kercheval and his fiancée to stay. I recognised him at once as Cliff Barnes from *Dallas* and I was overwhelmed with excitement. Ken had come to see Orston Church where the ancient name of Kercheval is carved in the porch.

Their stay at Langar was a delight and the next year the couple returned to have their marriage blessed in Orston Church. It was a lovely sunny day and I regret that I did not attend the ceremony.

I was probably too busy baking his favourite gooseberry pie. Nigel drove them to Church in a battered old Vauxhall Station wagon with a rusty roof rack on top. This completely flawed the press and waiting crowd who had gathered outside the church expecting something more traditional, like a stretch limousine

When my daughter Louise was working with me, I tried to persuade her to go on a course that the Tourist Board was running for struggling would-be hoteliers and the more experienced who needed help. I always hoped she might eventually enjoy it and decide to take over, but I'm glad now that her life took a completely different turn. The course was advertised as 'How to make money in catering without killing yourself' which appealed to me and, as Louise refused to spend her time in the North Nottingham Novotel, I signed myself up.

While I was imprisoned for three days and nights in the conference room, Louise was entertaining Dan Ackroyd, his brother Peter and their wild film crew.

The Blues Brother and his charming brother were delighted to find themselves in a private house with such a pretty waitress. Dan helped Louise light the fires and spent a morning cutting logs in the woodshed. A customer spotted him walking down the empty village street to the post office and told me later that he was so surprised to see Dan Ackroyd in such an unlikely environment that he thought he was hallucinating.

This lively group cheered us up and for a brief moment Louise almost found the business bearable.

In the late 1980s Central Television booked Bruno Brookes, at the height of his Radio 1 'disc jockey' fame, to stay for several weeks while he was hosting a show. I liked him very much and often sat up talking at the kitchen table, drinking vodka and orange. He told me about his life and his house in Ireland and gave me one good piece of advice: "When you're tired and fed up, remember the four letter word you take to the bank – cash."

Early one freezing cold morning, Bruno took me with him to visit the Newark antique fair. His driver had the limousine warmed up in readiness, we swept up to the gates without having to trudge from the car park, stall holders greeted him as we marched around and, when we were too cold, he rang his driver on the first mobile phone I ever saw. This was my introduction to the best part of how other people live and I was really impressed. Bruno always came in late and left late in the mornings in order to avoid the time spent in make up. Unfortunately this gave Langar Hall a rather bad reputation with the girls at Central Television who dealt with the bookings.

Our reputation with those girls suffered irretrievably after Michael Elphick stayed when he was filming *Boon* at locations around Nottinghamshire. They shot an episode at Langar, Polly the parrot made a sulky appearance in one scene while another gave the impression that the house was on fire. I particularly enjoyed the catering bus where I went every day for bacon butties.

Michael and his sidekick Neil Morrisey were great favourites, and I admired Michael as a pretty good actor. Vodka and orange late into the night featured heavily as we thoroughly enjoyed ourselves after filming.

Neil Morrisey returned a couple of times for a break. His television career had only just begun and it took me some time to recognise him in *Men Behaving Badly*. He used to have long dark hair and was always very nice about Langar and my way of running the hotel. Now he has his own hotel in Somerset which has many accolades and wins prizes for being the best.

Frankie Howard stayed with his crew shortly before he died, when he was performing at the Cotgrave miner's welfare centre. He suffered from acute stage fright which he relieved by shouting at his entourage. They had tense pre-performance briefings in the Study and I waited outside, ready to administer some efficacious brandy as they came out, one by one, white-faced and shaking.

Frankie Howard's show was an enormous success. Afterwards, confidence restored, he joined other guests to see Crispin's current after dinner play performed in the dining room. Frankie came to life. He loved the play and afterwards complimented the actors on their performance and for having the nerve to play so close to their audience.

After he left, I wished I had been able to tell him how much I loved *Up Pompeii*.

Another guest who I might have expected to be difficult was Ken Bates. I never read the sports pages of a newspaper and, knowing nothing about football, had no idea who he was. I loved him and his partner Susanne from the moment they walked through the door. It was half past one and as we did not serve lunch at that time, I was on my own in the house. I asked them politely if they had eaten, hoping they would say yes. I was rather thrown when Ken said "Thank you, we'd love something to eat, anything, just a sandwich."

So, parking Ken and Susanne in the Study with a bottle of Champagne, I scurried about the kitchen. There was no decent sliced bread but I found some terrine, smoked salmon and half a lobster, which I put on a big plate with some salad, added a loaf of Langar bread and a whole Stilton. I placed it on the Study table and they were delighted.

It proved to me that people used to the best hotels and restaurants appreciative simplicity, especially if the service comes from the heart.

Ken asked me if I had Fernet Branca, which I had never even heard of but I bought a bottle in Bingham that afternoon ready for when they returned from the match. We became friends for life! Ken drank peach schnapps with Champagne in the day and a large glass of Fernet Branca before he went to bed.

Taking a leaf from his book, we now do a mean peach schnapps cocktail for weddings and parties, using sparkling wine with Archers and perhaps a dash of gin if we feel the party needs livening up. Fernet Branca is handed out to favoured guests in need of a cure for a hangover; recently I discovered it is a brilliant pick-me-up when I feel too tired to face a busy dinner service. It is bitter medicine but it works wonders.

Before I even thought of taking in guests, I went on one of John Tovey's cookery courses at the Miller Howe Hotel at Windermere. Later, this charismatic chef came to stay at Langar on his way to visit Delia Smith. I was there on my own to welcome, cook and serve him. The meal was edible but not brilliant. I gave him kedgeree, which he insisted on eating again for breakfast. He gave me good advice which, had I always followed, would have saved me from some of the bad times. Flattering me that I was a 'natural with people', he told me to "stay out front and keep a close eye on the kitchen." I certainly carry that out now.

Tony Francis was another well-known face in the 1980s and 90s when he often appeared on television sports programmes. He had an office a mile away at Barnstone where he first worked on his programme *Heart of the Country* and has helped me enormously over the past ten and more years. When he first stayed at Langar Hall, I used to hide him away in the Study for privacy but he soon preferred to be part of the scene and chose to join the crowd.

He gave me a copy of his book *Tales from The Heart of the Country* in which he describes one occasion he stayed:

It wasn't so much the lack of a bedroom key that caught me off guard, as the appearance of a complete stranger beside my dressing table in the middle of the night. The ghost of Langar Hall? Not exactly - just an errant guest who had had one too many brandies and had forgotten his room number. Quite a baptism.

He filmed three television documentaries at Langar. The first was Crispin's Laurel and Hardy one- man show which he described as:

The stuff of legends, with Crispin 'the roly-poly supply teacher-cum-wine waiter-cum-entertainer' indeed several people squashed into one. A better off-the-cuff pianist and songwriter would be difficult to find. And his impersonation of Laurel and Hardy to his own accompaniment was quite brilliant. He was Oliver Hardy. Why he didn't go on to become a star I shall never know.

On another occasion, he recalls making a documentary of the first wedding to take place at Langar Hall:

May did us proud with a breathtakingly beautiful day. The hawthorn was in fragrant blossom and cow parsley fringed the croquet lawn with its lace-like whiteness. At that moment, I couldn't think of a finer place to get married. The only fly in the ointment was the arrival of a sewage truck to empty the septic tank. Burly men in boiler suits leaped from the wagon, brandishing hose reels as though they'd been invited to the reception. It's the only time I've seen Imogen blanche.

When he filmed carp fishing in the moat, 80-year-old Fred cooked a beautiful big fish under a chestnut tree and served it in the garden - smoked, fried or grilled. Afterwards, countless people asked if there was Langar carp on the menu. But although our carp taste like Dover sole when fresh, and there are far too many of them, I just can't bear to take their lives. Not even for 100% profit.

Sir Cliff Richard arrived one afternoon when I was not expecting him. When a tall, thin, dark-haired 'young' man got out of the back of a truck with a group of plump middle-aged Christian ladies, I did not recognise him. Then, when we realised who he was, 'us grannies' in the office went wild with excitement. We knew all the words of *We're all going on a Summer Holiday* and *Living Doll* which we sang in the kitchen to educate the techno chefs.

Cliff was modest and unassuming. He brought the Christian ladies back for a late supper in the restaurant to the delight of lingering diners and walked, unconcerned, through the dining room at lunchtime the next day. News of his visit spread the gospel of Langar Hall all over Nottinghamshire.

I was a great fan of *To The Manor Born* and empathised with Audrey Forbes Hamilton, so it is always fun when Penelope Keith and her husband come to stay. Her plays usually run for a week at the Theatre Royal in Nottingham, so there is plenty of time for good discussions.

Janet Street Porter presented a television programme walking from Edinburgh to Greenwich along the Greenwich Meridian line which runs directly through Reception and out through the Study windows. I found her quite difficult at first, but once settled with friends in the Study, she was all smiles.

On the day they filmed the Langar bit, the film crew lost her. When they caught up along the lane she gave them such a load of abuse that a passing car, witnessing her fury, stopped the crew's Land Rover and threatened to report them to the police. The driver took some time to be convinced that it was all the other way round. Meanwhile, I handed round so much Dr Bach's Rescue Remedy to the nervous young producers, and had taken enough myself to keep me calm, that I earned a cherished two-minute appearance on the programme.

Brian Johnson was the first cricket commentator who found Langar Hall around 1988 and since then the BBC has booked the Radio 4 *Test Match Special* team in for every important Trent Bridge cricket match.

I look forward to their stay as one of the highlights of the year and refuse every other room booking during that week. They are highly individual characters kept neatly in order by Shilpa, a tiny attractive young lady of Indian origin (always popular with me) who has never been to her ancestral home. Shilpa has a difficult job and there is usually some 'incident' during their stay that duly gets recorded on the radio or in one of the many books that these ex-cricketers write.

The TMS team work together in small cramped commentary boxes, flying off to India, Pakistan, Australia and countries all over the world where cricket is played, so they get to know each other all to well. Their natural good manners, shared passion for cricket and public school humour comes across on the radio and has won them many faithful followers.

They have brought many famous cricket names to Langar: Fred Truman, Clive Lloyd, Graham Gouch, Foxy Fowler and others. I can almost feel my father smiling down from the heavenly clouds.

Henry Blofeld, the 'voice of cricket', ranks as one of my all time favourites in the guest league. He is one of those rare proper old-fashioned, old Etonian gents - a dying breed of real charmers. His life has been threatened with a pattern of disasters that would flaw most people, but he never mentions the catastrophes unless asked and then passes over them lightly, with a laugh against himself. He is great company and tells marvellous stories. I have a few Blofeld stories myself.

One summer's night he was dining late and alone. At another table, a young man, keen to impress his new girl friend, was most upset when we ran out of lobsters. I suggested langoustines as an alternative before realising we had run out of them too. This was a bad start and the young man was rather cross. As his silent meal came to an end, he spotted Henry Blofeld at a nearby table and invited him to join them for a glass of wine. Henry is always up for the company of a pretty girl and stopped at their table on his way out of the dining room. A bottle or two later, they were getting along fine and it seemed the success of the evening was retrieved. Then, when the young man went to visit the gents, Henry invited the girl to dinner the following night.

I knew nothing about this so I was surprised when she turned up the following evening promptly at 8pm. I rang Henry in his room to tell him she was downstairs. He had entirely forgotten the invitation and was 'stumped'!

Henry writes with ease and humour, always has a book on the go and gives me a signed copy when it is published. I particularly like the one where Langar Hall gets a page and he describes me accurately:

> She trained at the school of benevolent and mildly absent-minded despots. She runs the hotel too beautifully and, in spite of her delightfully inconsequential air, she is firmly in control of everything, and anyone who doubts this does so at their peril. Langar has the wonderful atmosphere of the best sort of well lived in, largish country house where it all seems a little bit haphazard but nothing is left to chance.

I am not sure quite how to take that! Henry goes on to recount a very funny story of how the night porter mistook him for a taxi driver.

We have a room named Cricketers and the 'Hut' on the croquet lawn is called Agnew's after Jonathan Agnew or 'Aggers'. He wanted to stay for the night of a friend's wedding but as there was no room left for him and his gorgeous wife Emma, I promised to renovate the Hut. I had abandoned the idea of sleeping there myself; it was too small and when I wanted a sleep in the afternoon, croquet-playing guests were always looking in. There was just enough time before the wedding date to give it a good makeover. 'Aggers' supplied his Coat of Arms to hang above the door: stumps with two cricket bats crossed.

The Cartland Room is named after Barbara Cartland who used to stay with us on her way from Scotland to her home in Hampshire. This annual event always took place just after August Bank Holiday. She arrived with her two sons, her white Pekinese and her son's black Labrador, in a white Mercedes with a distinctive turquoise stripe.

A brandy in her room revived her after the long journey. She always came down dressed for dinner in pink or turquoise and enjoyed her food. Other guests fell silent as they enjoyed her conversation.

"No I don't want to go to Thailand on holiday. Last time I was there, I stayed with the King. An hotel would be dull in comparison."

She was staying the night after Princess Diana died. The telephone went mad with the media wanting interviews. She loved all that but I suspect her comments were unprintable as nothing was published. Her opinion of the Royal Family was controversial and I gathered there was a feud, which may have dated back to when she was not invited to Princess Diana's wedding. I think she had cause to feel slighted as the step-grandmother-in-law.

On her last visit, she wore no make up. Her skin, habitually plastered in white foundation and false lashes stuck together with green mascara, was as clear and fresh as a young girl's. She walked up the stairs unaided, lay on her bed in an 'Eleanor Glynn' attitude and said: "Let's have a gossip."

Barbara was outspoken and as she was rather deaf, the gossip was one-sided. Instead of her usual bubbly chat, she spoke sadly about the husband, brothers, father and friends who were killed in the war.

"Oxford Street is full of Germans these days. What do you think?" (No pause) "Every where you go in London, Germans, Germans, Germans." A few months later she joined her loved ones. I was really sorry that she did not make her hundredth birthday although I felt she had had enough of the life she had made for herself and lived to the full.

I always longed for a paparazzi experience. The nearest I got was through *Daily Mirror* reporter Ted Oliver who used Langar Hall as a sanctuary for people whose scandalous stories had recently appeared in the paper and who he needed to hide away. Once, he was interviewing an IRA 'super-grass' who had been smuggled into the country by M15 and hidden in Radcliffe on Trent. On another occasion he brought what I thought was a perfectly ordinary family – father, mother and child. I never quite understood the details but it was something to do with the father being really the mother after a sex change, though goodness knows who the mother was. The father, perhaps?

When *Coronation Street* actress Sarah Lancashire and the head of BBC TV, Peter Salmon, chose to get married at Langar, wanting a quiet, informal family wedding, I did everything I could to keep it secret. But when the day arrived, I simply longed for paparazzi and there they were, parked at the end of the drive with French security men to prevent anyone coming closer. It was a hot day in August, so I used the excuse to take trays of water, larger and lemonade to the waiting Press. They were bored, and as they had nothing better to do, they interviewed me before 'Racquel' and Peter came down the drive for their brief photo call. I was thrilled to see myself on *Central News* and *ITN News At Ten* that night. Again, great publicity for Langar Hall.

Other celebrities who have stayed at Langar include Jules Holland and Jack Dee who come when their tours take them to Nottingham. I love their visits and like to go in to the Study for a brief chat, while keeping others out - one of the perks of being the owner! One morning at breakfast, I was complaining so much about Christmas that I actually made Jack Dee laugh. Well, just a little laugh.

Like many Nottingham people who were around in the late 1960s, I am very proud to know the fashion designer Sir Paul Smith. He used to have a shop in Bridlesmith Gate called 'The Bird Cage' when Andrew and I had a picture gallery up the road in Byard Lane. Being extremely small in those days, even size 8 was too big for me. Paul made me some lovely clothes that I wish I still had. Strange though it may seem in a house full of antiques and works of art, those clothes are the only things that have been stolen.

When he first stayed at Langar, Paul was a well-known designer, renowned for his suits. I remember him coming into the White Sitting Room and introducing himself:

"Hello Imogen. I think we met in 1886."

He remembers the White Sitting Room when it was white, since when it slowly became increasingly coloured. Recently, Paul asked sheepishly if I would mind if he changed the room a bit. One hour and a quarter later he had transformed it back to its original tranquillity. Hot colours went upstairs, cool colours came down. A pale rug was found in the barn, a sofa bought in a sale in Bingham, a cover chosen for another. I learned from him how to fit a day's work into a few hours. Just get up and get on with it. Seize the minute.

I have learnt a lot more from Paul. He has been a huge influence on me and on Langar Hall and I take any advice he offers and act on it immediately. He was rather concerned when I was planning to extend the Study and build the bar. When he looked out of the Indian room window onto a blank wall, he pointed out that the new bar made that part of the house claustrophobic. It needed a window.

As soon as his team of designers arrived to brainstorm their next collection he sent them off to design the window, the results of which we put in to good effect. When the bar was at last up and running but my decor left much to be desired, he sent a team to hang the walls with his collection of photographs. And so it became the Paul Smith bar. This is just another of the countless ways he has helped and encouraged me over the past ten years. It is greatly thanks to him that I have kept the house very much as it was. He understands my original concept and his opinion gave me the confidence to stick to my guns when professional catering advice was to the contrary.

Over the years I have watched Paul grow into an international star with a huge business in Japan as well as shops in Paris, London and New York. I love his clothes and like to wear them myself when I can fit into them.

Sir Paul's PA, Colette, keeps him together and we both love to cherish her. They work hard when they are here but still find time to go to the post office to buy scratch cards or play on the swings or go for a spin in my car. I enjoy the days when the team of young designers comes to work in the Study. They are surprisingly modest and unaffected by success. Could it be that they take their boss as an example?

As long as Paul is in business, using Nottingham as his base, I shall ensure that his rooms and the Study are always available for him.

CHAPTER THIRTEEN

Guides

If I failed to get the Guide ratings that I thought Langar Hall deserved, I had only myself to blame. I read the rulebooks and, without being economical with the truth, I ticked all the right boxes. But when it came to the interviews with the inspectors, the morning after their anonymous stay, I used to argue impatiently. They didn't like the study and since that is my most popular room, I took their criticism badly. For years our accolades remained annoyingly low.

Then one day, before I left on my annual holiday to India, I had a brilliant idea.

I promoted Richard, who was head of reception and organised the weddings and parties, to General Manager, kitted him out in a Paul Smith suit and wrote a letter for him to sign and post to the AA and Michelin guides:

> Dear Sir, I have recently taken over as General Manager of Langar Hall and I am surprised that an establishment of this standard is not more highly rated…I would be delighted to discuss the problem with you on your next visit etc.etc.…

The plot worked. While 'the cross little old lady and her mad druggy chef' were safely out of the way, we got our second AA rosette for the food and third star for the hotel. I was well pleased.

The *Michelin Guide* is a harder fish to fry. I longed for just the smallest mention in the Guide, not a star but perhaps a knife and fork beside our entry in recognition of good food. But although horrid hotels where I would never dream of staying get a mention, Langar Hall was black-balled until Richard's letter attracted the second inspector in 15 years.

A tweedy young man arrived on a Monday night, Toby's training night in the kitchen, when three local lads, all under 20, cooked the dinner. The dining room was quite busy, and the inspector, who of course I had not spotted, seemed satisfied. In the morning, just as he revealed his identity, Richard arrived looking every inch the capable manager. I kept quiet and did not argue about anything at all.

The Michelin man departed happily, warning us to expect a visit from other inspectors who would come incognito, in all kinds of disguises. It seemed we were in with a chance and determined to be extra courteous to all the guests, just in case.

Then one Friday we took a last minute booking for a man on his own. It is rare to have single bookings after Thursday night when the businessmen go home, so surely this must be The Inspector?

We gave him the best available room, flowers checked, bed turned down. He arrived late and went straight to the coveted corner table in the dining room. He ordered rum and coke. Well perhaps he was tired of all the fine wine he had drunk at 'work' around the best hotels. He ate appreciatively without comment. After dinner he went down to the pub. Again I thought this was a nice way for him to relax and as he had not returned by the time I went to bed, I told Roy the night porter to look out for him and give him whatever he asked for when he returned.

Long past midnight, a big farmer from the village carried the 'inspector' back to the house and dumped him in Reception. Roy politely asked him if there was anything he needed.

"Yes. A bottle of Jack Daniels and a woman," he replied, producing a call girl card from his pocket. Roy took the card with the number and telephoned Toby for help. There was a scuffle when Roy refused to hand over a bottle of Jack Daniels before Toby appeared wearing only his Indian longhi, which looks rather like a skirt. The inspector took fright and incontinently peed on the tiled floor. My help was now needed; called from my bed, I came on the scene in a white flannel nightdress looking like a tiny ghost.

The poor man was legless and confused. He wanted to go home. Apologising for 'the accident' he produced a thick wad of notes and told me to keep it all to cover his bill. I resisted the temptation, counted enough to cover dinner and called a taxi.

When Richard came in early next morning, ready to do the interview, every one had a good laugh. After that, any suspicion we had that a customer might be from the *Michelin Guide* became a joke. We had learnt our lesson and as far as I'm aware there were no more visits.

Although I complain about the Guides, they have been very helpful. How else would I have known about all those details that customers expect? They lay down the rules and it's pointless to ignore them.

My favourite guides are *The Good Hotel Guide* and *The Good Food Guide*. You don't pay to be included, customers write up and recommend you. My customers started writing from the start, before I knew about the books. So when someone booked saying that he had found us in *The Good Hotel Guide*, I felt I had to tell him that we were neither good nor a hotel. He came anyway and stayed on a regular basis.

The only award we ever won was for the 'Most highly enjoyable, mildly eccentric Good Hotel of the Year 2000.' I went with Toby to the award party and proudly collected our plaque. The other winners, and there were many categories, were surprisingly modest unassuming people. I expected, being in the people trade, they would be gregarious, perhaps drink a bit too much. Anyway I was soon bored standing around looking at my glass so I set off to 'work the room,' introducing myself. I longed to meet and get to know a few fellow hoteliers and I was surprised that they were not party people. That was probably because they were always giving parties for other people. They were professional. I bet there were no spiders in their corners or flies in the soup.

Perhaps that was the point when I realised it was time to take another quantum leap and change for the better.

The *Caterer and Hotel Keeper* trade magazine, which is published weekly, has been another source of education. I read it as soon as it arrives on Thursday mornings along with *Country Life* and the *Oldie*.

This magazine 'adopts' a business, follows its progress through the year, reporting on its success and failures. I love to read about other people's disasters and dismiss all those business plans and profit forecasts with derision.

When Toby spotted that the *Caterer & Hotelkeeper* was advertising for new businesses to adopt, he insisted that I put our name forward.

"But we've been going for years, they only want a new business. They only do new businesses." I was horrified

But there is no point in arguing with Toby so, late that night, I typed a letter to the editor. I made up a story saying that although we were not a new business; we were going to start again professionally. A conventional management structure was to take the place of crisis management. We were building on a bar, refurbishing rooms and bathrooms and goodness knows what other sensible ideas I dreamed up.

A few months later Forbes Much, the editor, whose parents just happened to live locally, called in to see me. I was embarrassed and kept apologising for my misleading letter. I explained that it was unlikely that I would be able to carry out any of the plans I mentioned. Then I introduced him to Jan. She had all the figures he needed at her fingertips, including my 'psychic chart' which we have kept since 1988. (In April I guess how much we will take each month, pencil the figure beside last year's column and we are seldom more than £500 out)

Months later I dreamt that I had let myself in for riding in the Grand National and I was absolutely terrified. Gordon Richards produced the kit and a horse while I planned how to start after the other horses and jump off before the first fence without hurting myself. When I realised I would have to get on the horse in the paddock, in full view of the public, I woke up, heart pounding with fear.

When the telephone rang the following afternoon, I answered with the same feeling of fear overwhelming me. It was the *Caterer & Hotelkeeper* with the news that they had chosen Langar Hall. Wasting no time, I immediately got planning

I had to do something that would make good reading. I employed Lynette Coyne to give the bedrooms a make over and plans went ahead to build the new bar. The kitchen brigade went up to seven and I employed some good French staff to back up Michael. Richard and Jan took care of the new management structure. But I did not hand over my role in the restaurant.

Jan was able to produce the necessary figures without any trouble and I wrote the basis of the monthly articles before Noella, a beautiful blond Irish journalist arrived by train from London. Noella was a party girl with a turbulent love life. We got on well and I did not mind if she only came in time for lunch before rushing back to deal with her romances. I had written her article in advance; she only had to change it into her own words

The whole experience shocked me out of my complacency and by the last instalment we had indeed blossomed into a credible hotel with a prospering restaurant and a turnover of £1 million.

CHAPTER FOURTEEN

The Future

I took my eight year old grand daughter, Leela, to see The Lion King last summer. She watched entranced, carried away by the dancing, music and colours. At the end I asked her if she would like to be a dancer when she grew up.

"Of course not Granny, you know what I want to do."

"What darling?" How could I have even momentarily forgotten?

"I want to run Langar when you are old and rule it myself when you are dead."

Great! . Now all I have to do is to live to be a lively 75 when she will be 18 and then drift along gently before booking into that heavenly hotel in the sky.

Born on the Queen Mother's birthday (a very good omen), Leela has the delicate beauty of her Anglo Indian birth. She and I share the same Leo star sign and we are both single-minded and determined.

I think Leela is tougher than I am. She should be just the ticket.

On the way home Leela offered her brother Alfie a job. Alfie is a real charmer aged six

"I don't want to be Leela's servant," he protested. "I'm going to be the gardener."

Well that's settled then.

Langar is such an extraordinarily lovely corner of England. Nothing spectacular, just the gentle beauty of green fields, ancient trees and walks around a pattern of water, low hills in the distance. I never fail to be overwhelmed by a feeling of love for everything as I wander along the grassy paths and look up to see the deep ochre painted house by the honey coloured stone church.

My father gave me a present for life as well as a life when he handed it over to me all those years ago and I am deeply grateful. It seemed unlikely then that I would be able to leave it in as good, if not better condition than when I took over. Now even the garden is flourishing and for the first time in a hundred years the path at the back of the moat is clear and there is a boat on the water. There could be another lifetime's satisfaction creating a garden there.

Meanwhile I am already working on the next five-year plan. It starts with marketing which I now realise is important, so I'll begin with re-branding as a Restaurant with Rooms. That may stop complaints from a few hotel guests who find the house too crowded with people and parties at the weekend.

In a couple of year's time, I would like to build an orangery along the south side of the house, with French windows from the study and the White Sitting Room. I know just the man to design it, a favourite customer of course, and we have already made a start with a few drawings on the tablecloths when he comes to dinner.

It will be a pleasant space to sit with a few tables that I could use for people dropping in for a really good snack menu served all day from noon till midnight. Not very large; just the same width as the one that used to be there before the war, but longer.

Meanwhile the outside of the house and the lodge need painting again, the same yellow ochre colour wash, and next winter the ha-ha will have to be rebuilt to keep the sheep out.

I am often asked what I am going to do when I retire. Retire? If I could get two days off a week and two months holiday a year I think I could go on forever. The two months is fairly easy. Two days seems impossible, there is always someone coming to lunch or dinner I really want to see. So, for the moment I'm going to <u>do</u> nothing. I'll just carry on as long as my health holds out and there are people still willing to work here and people still happy to come to visit Langar to keep it alive and prospering.

I love living here so I won't move far. Perhaps just five yards from the kitchen door where I could take over the whole of the stable block. When I'm really old and feeble I could ring a bell for food and keep a huge drink cupboard in my sitting room and entertain my old friends when they book in for lunch.

My daughter Louise will inherit the property. I can trust her to make the right decisions when the time comes. She and Toby are very close and I know he will help her as he has helped me. I hope they will be able to keep the place for Leela and Alfie.

Louise and I get on surprisingly well together and I wonder how she turned out to be such a nice person. She is honest and kind, funny and fair. Quite strict too, with me as well as her children.

Today, in these uncertain times, I could not wish to pass on to my family anything more precious than this lovely, adaptable house which has proved capable of bringing in an income to finance its upkeep and a living for whoever is lucky enough to live here. If life gets hard, there is a well and good land to grow vegetables

I don't think too much about the future any more. I'll think about that tomorrow.

Who would have guessed what has happened to Langar Hall in the last 20 years? Certainly not me! My old family home, slowly and hesitantly evolved into a restaurant, while I reluctantly grew into a 'serious' restaurateur.

"Yesterday is but a dream, tomorrow but a vision. But today well lived makes every yesterday a dream of happiness, and every tomorrow a vision of hope."

Sanskrit proverb

(Langar is the Sanskrit word for a place where pilgrims receive hospitality.)